REVIEWS OF OTHER BOOKS BY SEAN GABB

"Fascinating to read, very well written,
an intriguing plot and I enjoyed it very much."
(Derek Jacobi, star of *I Claudius* and *Gladiator*)

"Vivid characters, devious plotting and buckets of gore
are enhanced by his unfamiliar choice of period.
Nasty, fun and educational."
(*The Daily Telegraph*)

"He knows how to deliver a fast-paced story and his grasp of the
period is impressively detailed."
(*The Mail on Sunday*)

"A rollicking and raunchy read . . . Anyone who enjoys their history
with large dollops of action, sex, intrigue and, above all, fun will
absolutely love this novel."
(*Historical Novels*)

"As always, [his] plotting is as brilliantly devious as the mind of his
sardonic and very earthy hero. This is a story of villainy that reels
you in from its prosaic opening through a series of death-defying
thrills and spills."
(*The Lancashire Evening Post*)

"It would be hard to over-praise this extraordinary series,
a near-perfect blend of historical detail and atmosphere
with the plot of a conspiracy thriller, vivid characters, high
philosophy and vulgar comedy."
(*The Morning Star*)

STORIES FROM PAUL THE DEACON

A LATIN READER FOR GCSE, A-LEVEL AND UNIVERSITY STUDENTS

EDITED WITH AN INTRODUCTION, NOTES AND COMPREHENSIVE VOCABULARY

by
SEAN GABB

CAS

CENTRE FOR ANCIENT STUDIES
DEAL
MMXVIII

Stories from Paul the Deacon: A Latin Reader for GCSE, A-Level and University Students, by Sean Gabb

First edition published in June 2018

© *Sean Gabb, 2018*

ISBN-13: 978-1719512596
ISBN-10: 1719512590

Published by:

The Centre for Ancient Studies
73 Middle Street
Deal, Kent CT14 6HN
England

Telephone: 07956 472 199
sean@seangabb.co.uk
www.seangabb.co.uk
www.classicstuition.co.uk

I Dedicate This Book
to my dear Wife Andrea
and to my Daughter Philippa

TABLE OF CONTENTS

ADDRESS TO THE READER

Introduction

The purpose of this book is to give students a set of readings that are in genuine but fairly simple Latin, and that are interesting in themselves, and that are accompanied by a Vocabulary in which nearly every word used in the text is fully explained. I hope it will be useful to GCSE and A-Level students, and to undergraduates who are beginning an accelerated course in Latin. Nor do I forget students in home-education or those who are trying to learn Latin by themselves.

One of the difficulties that students of Latin at any level face is a lack of reading material that is both original and accessible. Both qualities are important. For beginners, the second of these is probably more important. If you have learned—even perhaps memorised—the grammar and rules of syntax, you have not yet learned Latin. If you are able to read a sentence by looking for the main verb, and then any subject, and then their dependent parts, you have still not learned Latin. You have learned only how to decode. You have learned the language when you are able to read an entire passage, quickly and accurately, without being consciously aware of the rules you are applying. This is an ability that comes from several hundred hours of practice—practice with texts that are not of forbidding complexity.

Now, there is, for beginners, no shortage of written material. I think, for example, of the excellent *Latin Stories* by Cullen, Dormandy and Taylor. The texts are both easy and interesting. They allow vocabulary to be learned and habits of understanding to be absorbed almost without conscious effort. They take a reader who has mastered the basics of grammar and syntax, and finish somewhat beyond the level required by the latest GCSE specification. Here, though, the guiding hand is largely withdrawn.

At A-Level, if the unseen texts are hardly beyond the level of *Latin Stories*, the prescribed texts are in entirely genuine Latin—and these can, at this stage, be of forbidding complexity. The classical writers did not set out to be accessible even to their own average contemporaries. Going to them straight from GCSE is rather like trying to clean windows from a ladder too short for their height. It can be done, with much standing on tiptoe, and much outstretching of arms. But Cicero's *Pro Milone* is more often started than finished. So too Book VIII of *The Aeneid*, and the various other texts currently prescribed. Not surprisingly, many students at A-Level give up on direct engagement, preferring to memorise the texts together with their translations.

I have prepared this book with these students largely in mind. As a writer, Paul the Deacon (c.720-799) stands at a level intermediate between *Latin Stories* and the Roman classics. A further advantage is that the extracts given here are in entirely genuine Latin. Turn forward to any of the texts, and you are reading the unaltered prose of a man whose working language was Latin. Paul is a writer of much enthusiasm and curiosity. He is lucid and often graceful, and variously learned and sceptical and colloquial. He has a grim sense of humour, and a sense of history. He knows how to tell a story, and how to weave his stories into an extended narrative. He is justly called the Herodotus of the Middle Ages.

Though I have an obvious bias, I think he is as enjoyable as Livy, and he shows a greater respect for the truth than Tacitus. All this you can know for yourself, sure that no editor has been through it, changing words here and there, or stripping out subordinate clauses. In short, I give you a master of Latin prose who, without tampering, can be read and appreciated with an intermediate knowledge of Latin. To go back to my analogy of the window cleaner, this book adds another half-dozen rungs to the ladder.

So much for A-Level. What of GCSE? My answer is that, if somewhat beyond, Paul is not too far beyond the level required. If you are studying Latin at GCSE not just for another set of points towards your university application, but as a path into one of the most interesting and abundant of all literatures, I can think of few writers more suitable than Paul the Deacon. All that I have said above still applies. Put in the minimum effort to read him, and it will be hard to emerge from the GCSE without a Level 9.

As for university and other students, I have probably said enough already. But Paul is genuine. He is accessible. He is interesting. I do defy anyone to start on one of the passages selected, and not to want to finish it, and not to want to move to the next.

The Language

There is an old prejudice, dating from the Renaissance, against the Latin authors of the Middle Ages. They are said to write of childish things, and in an obscure and barbarous jargon. They are despised for failing to write exactly like Cicero and Tacitus. This is an absurd prejudice. What we call *Mediaeval Latin* was written for about a thousand years, beginning perhaps in the fourth century, with Saint Jerome's translation of The Bible. As with any other language, it was used by writers of limited understanding, but also by writers of genius. If it was not usually written in exactly the style of the Latin classics, that is because a language changes over time. New words are needed to express new ideas, or old words are put to new uses. Styles of composition change to accommodate new mental habits, or to reach out to new audiences.

But, to focus on the present writer, I do not think Paul's *Historia Langobardorum* would have been meaningless to Livy. Certainly, Paul had received an excellent education in the Roman classics, and he knew some Greek. If I have marked in my footnotes some of the main departures from classical usage, the difference in Latin between Livy and Paul is no greater than the difference in English between John Milton and John Bunyan. We do not sneer at either English writer because he failed to write like the other. If we must, we should regard Paul as more rungs on the ladder towards the Roman classics. If we can, we should enjoy him for himself.

As said, I have supplied a dictionary that covers nearly every word used in the text. For some students, I have no doubt this will be excessive. Do you really need to be told the meaning of *binus* and *digredior*? For others, this will justify the price of the book. The whole meaning of a passage can often be lit up by finding the meaning of one unknown word; and it is useful to have both text and dictionary between one set of covers. Even with a good knowledge of Word for Windows, and some of Visual Basic, compiling the dictionary was a laborious task, and I hope it will be useful to someone.

As for the notes, I have tried to strike a balance between leaving readers to work out for themselves the details of a period that is largely unknown outside a handful of university departments, and making every name of a person or place into a small essay. I give a short reading list at the end of this Address. Or there is Wikipedia. One of the open secrets of modern education is that students are warned not to use this, and are penalised if they reference it. Yet everyone, teachers as well as students, uses it. I agree that, if you are researching Donald Trump, or anything about the Middle East, Wikipedia at any one moment is a snapshot of a dispute between rival teams of fanatics. But, if you want to know how the Lombards conquered Italy, or how Constans II tried to take it back, what you find on Wikipedia is probably reliable. Otherwise, I will now give a short background to Paul's *History* that will be useful to anyone whose knowledge becomes hazy after the death of Augustus and only sharpens again at the Battle of Bosworth Field.

Historical Background

In 395, following a century of experiment, the Roman Empire was divided into Eastern and Western administrative zones, with joint Emperors in Rome and in Constantinople. The purpose was to let each Emperor deal with the pressure on his own critical frontiers—the barbarians along the Rhine and Danube frontiers in the West, and the Persians along the Euphrates and desert frontiers in the East.

In theory, each Emperor was equal. In practice, the Eastern Emperor, ruling from Constantinople, was soon the senior partner. During the next two hundred years, becoming increasingly Greek in language in culture, the Eastern Empire flourished, and Constantinople became one of the largest and most opulent cities in the world.

The Western Empire went into immediate and rapid decline. In 406, barbarians crossed the Rhine in large numbers, and broke into Italy. In 410, they sacked Rome. By then, the Western Capital had been moved to Ravenna, a city in North Eastern Italy, impregnable behind marshes, and within easy reach of the frontiers—and within easier reach of Constantinople.

During the next seventy years, the Barbarians took France and Spain and North Africa from the Empire. Britain remained in the Empire, but its people were told to look to their own defence. In 476, the last Western Emperor was deposed. By 500, the whole of the Western Empire had been replaced by a patchwork of barbarian kingdoms.

After 527, the Emperor Justinian began to reach out from Constantinople to reconquer the lost Western provinces. He recovered North Africa and Italy and part of Spain. However, the effort was exhausting. After his death in 568, the Empire lost much of Italy to the Lombard barbarians, and Rome itself fell under papal domination. Slavic and Avar barbarians crossed the Danube and conquered and burned all the way to Athens and the walls of Constantinople. After 602, the Persians began a war of destruction against the Empire. Though they ultimately lost, they did briefly take Egypt and Syria.

The Persians suffered total defeat by the Empire in the 620s. This did not lead to an age of restored peace. Instead, the chaos of the war, plus environmental changes that I mention without discussing, allowed the first eruption of Islam. Once again, the Empire lost Egypt and Syria, now for good. This was not the end. Not only did the Empire manage what no else has—to fight Radical Islam to a halt—it also evolved into the Glory that was Mediaeval Byzantium. But this takes me outside the scope of my Historical Background.

Returning to Italy, this was, by 600, divided between the Empire and the Lombards, while the Papacy sat largely on the fence. Governed by an Exarch, or Viceroy, the remaining Imperial possessions in Italy had their capital in Ravenna, a city in the North. Because of the Emperor's preoccupation with the Persian and later with the Arab Wars, the Exarch was effectively his own man. He could rule and make war or peace as he pleased.

When the Lombards first entered Italy, they were a most savage race of barbarians. They were also highly intelligent. Unlike the Avars and the Huns, they destroyed only when they were resisted. Unlike the Ostrogoths, no amount of Imperial diplomacy or direct military action was enough to dislodge them. Within fifty years, they had converted to Christianity. Their higher classes had adopted both Latin and the wider Roman culture. Their ambition was to become the rulers of a Latin and Christian and prosperous Italy, more or less at peace with the Eastern Empire. Their capital was sometimes Pavia, another city in Northern Italy, and sometimes Milan.

Paul the Deacon

Paul the Deacon—known in Latin as Paulus Diaconus, and also called Paulus Casinensis, Paulus Levita, and Winfrid son of Warnefrid—was born some time about 720 at Fruili in North Eastern Italy. Leupichis, one of his ancestors, had entered Italy with Alboin in 568, and been granted lands close by Friuli. During the Avar invasion of c.611, the five sons of Leupchis were carried off into captivity. But one was able to return and continue the family line. His grandson, Warnfrid, married a certain Theudelinda, and their son was Paul.

He seems to have been educated at the court of King Ratchis in Pavia. Studying under Flavianus the Grammarian, he followed the Latin curriculum

5

standard to his age, but appears also to have learned Greek. We can presume that he was fluent in the language of his own people, though his first language may have been Latin, or whatever intermediary stage between this and Italian was commonly spoken in his day.

He may have been secretary to Desiderius, the next King of the Lombards. We know that he was tutor to the King's daughter, Adelperga. After Pavia was taken by Charlemagne in 774, he moved to the court of Duke Archis at Benevento. He then became a monk at Monte Cassino. In 782, he joined the court of Charlemagne, where, with Alcuin and Einhard, he played a distinguished part in the Carolingian revival of learning. He died on the 13th April, probably in 799.

His first literary work, produced at the request of Duchess Adelperga, was the *Historia Romana*, a revised and expanded version of Eutropius. To this he added two further books, carrying the history to the time of Justinian. Another of his works, *Liber de Episcopis Mettensibus*, is a history of the Bishops of Metz, which contains an account of the family and ancestors of Charlemagne. He composed numerous other works, both in prose and in verse.

His most important work is the *Historia Gentis Langobardorum Libri Sex*, known in English as *The History of the Lombards*. He wrote this in old age, and left it unfinished at his death. What we have, though, is a connected narrative of Lombard History from the earliest days in Scandinavia to 774, when the Lombard Kingdom was incorporated into the Empire of Charlemagne.

Paul's general theme is obvious. He tells how the Lombards, a people of exceptional courage and intelligence, move from the freezing wastes of the North in search of a better home. They leave behind them other barbarians of decidedly low quality. In their wanderings, they fight or join with other peoples. At last, they are *invited* into Italy—a dubious though a convenient claim—and take it for themselves. The Lombards are not like other barbarians. These are either little better than the beasts of the field, or they have a taste for gang-rape and impalement. They are not like the treacherous and degenerate Greeks. They rule for the most part justly, and are insensibly assimilated into the language and culture of the land. They protect the land from enemies who mean it nothing but ill.

You see this most clearly in Book V, the main part of which deals with the attempted reconquest of Italy by the Empire. This should be seen as Paul's counterpart to the Persian invasion in Herodotus. The contrast is at all times sharp between Western courage and honour and the degraded state of the East. Constans II arrives and asks for a blessing on his enterprise. He is told that the Lombards are the divinely-ordained rulers of Italy. He takes cities by siege—there is no suggestion that, as with the reconquest a century earlier by Justinian, the natives open their gates to welcome him. He visits Rome, where he is greeted politely by the Pope, but then strips the city of any metal that can be coined into money. He fails to overcome the Lombards, and withdraws to Sicily, where his tax-gatherers are outstandingly and unprecedentedly oppressive. He is finally murdered by his own domestics, and the Lombard areas of Italy are free to continue their development as part of a reviving West.

That Paul has an agenda is obvious. He is not, however, a crude propagandist. Alboin was the king who led his people into Italy. He spared the people of Pavia even after a siege of three years. Paul also describes him as a tyrant in his domestic arrangements, and his wife as loose with her favours. The Empire is mostly at war with the Lombards. Paul treats Constans harshly, but is able to admire and even praise other Emperors. Not every Lombard is shown as a saint, not every enemy as a villain. Paul is an unusual historian in his unwillingness to paint wholly white or black portraits of his characters.

The *Historia Langobardorum* is a work of greatness in its own right. It also testifies to a progress of which Paul himself was necessarily ignorant. The popular idea is that the Romans conquered the Empire because of their virtues, and lost it because of their vices. These vices were first sexual incontinence and a lack of honour, and then a corrupted version of Christianity that stopped them from holding the frontiers. The truth, it is increasingly plain, is that the Empire fell on evil times because of variations in the output of the Sun. By about 200, the world was moving into one of its cooling periods. This made agriculture less productive. It began a movement of disease-bearing rodents across the Eurasian landmass. The diseases then struck already weakened populations, reducing the number of taxpayers and potential soldiers, and generally sapping the foundations of high civilisation. At the same time, colder weather forced waves of primitive peoples from their own lands to the more temperate zones.

The effects of all this for China, Persia and the Roman Empire were all disastrous. There was a general collapse of population. Political and military incompetence, misgovernment—even outright treason—were but secondary causes of the disaster. The pagans tended to believe their fate was written in the stars. It does seem to have been written in the internal workings of our own star.

Paul's *History* covers the last phase of the cooling cycle. By the time he was born, global temperatures appear to have been recovering. The result for us was the birth of a new European civilisation. Rather than condemn the men of Paul's world for their superstition and frequent lack of culture, we should rather admire them for how they weathered the storm. Cities shrank. Technologies disappeared. But what could be saved was saved. Every attempt was made to keep some degree of civilised life in being. Paul lived long enough to join the first generation of what is called the Carolingian Renaissance—when, under the patronage of Charlemagne, crumbling books were pulled from their places of safety and copied. Many of these copies still exist. Hardly anything they saved has perished since then. Paul's life stands on the border between the age of preservation and the first age of revival. His writings are a monument in themselves, and a monument to the endurance of our civilisation.

If I can, through these extracts from his writings, help to improve the Latin of those who read them, I shall not have published in vain. If I can bring his writings to a wider audience of the appreciative, I shall not have taught in vain. I therefore commend Paul the Deacon and his *Historia Langobardorum*.

Sean Gabb
Centre for Ancient Studies
June 2018

Further Reading

The edition of the *Historia Langobardorum* from which I have mostly worked is by Waitz (Hanover, 1878). The is available in photographic pdf *via* the Internet Archive and Google Books.

The best account of Italy in this period is probably still Volume V of Thomas Hodgkin, *Italy and Her Invaders*, Oxford University Press, 1895. This too is available on-line.

Chapter LXVIII of Gibbon's *History of the Decline and Fall of the Roman Empire* (1776-87) remains of general use. As ever, this is available in multiple editions on-line.

Otherwise, I commend the novels of Richard Blake listed on the reverse front paper of this book. These cover events in Italy and the Empire during the early seventh century. That I am "Richard Blake" is surely irrelevant to my recommendation of his twelve historical novels....

THE LOMBARDS: A BRIEF CHRONOLOGY

All dates are *Anno Domini*

9—First mention of Lombards in Roman sources by Velleius Paterculus

487—Lombard migration to Danube Region

c 526—Reign of Lombard king Wacho; migration to Pannonia

542—First outbreak of bubonic plague in Constantinople

560—Alboin succeeds his father Audoin as King of the Lombards

565—Death of Justinian

567—Avars and Lombards ally to defeat the Gepids of Pannonia

568—Narses dismissed; Lombard invasion of Italy

572—Pavia surrenders; becomes Lombard capital

572—Alboin murdered by his wife

572-86—Individual Lombard dukes fight for control of the kingdom

586-90—Reign of King Authari

614—St Augustine converts the English

590-616—Reign of King Agilulf who strengthens the Lombard kingdom

602—Phocas becomes Emperor; beginning of Great Persian War

610—Execution of Phocas; Heraclius becomes Emperor

614—Jerusalem falls to the Persians

618—Loss of Egypt to the Persians

616-28—Reign of Queen Theudelinda of the Lombards

628—Final defeat of the Persians

634—Beginning of the Arab Conquests

628-36 Reign of King Adaloald

636-52 Reign of King Rothari

652-712—Lombard kingdom is divided between rule from Milan and rule from Pavia

663—Invasion of Italy by Constans II

668—Death of Constans II

668—First Arab siege of Constantinople; first use of Greek Fire to drive them off

717—Second Arab siege of Constantinople; driven off again with Greek Fire

c 720—Birth of Paul the Deacon

712-44 Reign of King Liutprand who unites the Kingdom of the Lombards

744-74—Decline of the Kingdom of the Lombards in Italy under ineffective rulers

774—Lombards defeated by Charlemagne of the Franks; Lombard Kingdom falls

c 799—Death of Paul the Deacon

800—Charlemagne crowned Holy Roman Emperor in Rome; a new age begins

HISTORY OF THE LOMBARDS

Germany: A Factory of Humanity

Septemtrionalis plaga quanto magis ab aestu solis remota est et nivali frigore gelida, tanto salubrior corporibus hominum et propagandis est gentibus coaptata; sicut econtra omnis meridiana regio, quo solis est fervori vicinior, eo semper morbis habundat et educandis minus est apta mortalibus.[1] Unde fit, ut tantae populorum multitudines arctoo sub axe oriantur, ut non inmerito universa illa regio Tanai tenus usque ad occiduum, licet et propriis loca in ea singula nuncupentur nominibus, generali tamen vocabulo Germania vocitetur; quamvis et duas ultra Rhenum provincias Romani, cum ea loca occupassent, superiorem inferioremque Germaniam dixerint. Ab hac ergo populosa Germania saepe innumerabiles captivorum turmae abductae meridianis populis pretio distrahuntur. Multae quoque ex ea, pro eo quod tantos mortalium germinat, quantos alere vix sufficit, saepe gentes egressae sunt, quae nihilominus et partes Asiae, sed maxime sibi contiguam Europam afflixerunt. Testantur hoc ubique urbes erutae per totam Illyricum Galliamque, sed maxime miserae Italiae, quae paene omnium illarum est gentium experta saevitiam. Gothi siquidem Wandalique, Rugi, Heruli atque Turcilingi, necnon etiam et aliae feroces et barbarae nationes e Germania prodierunt.[2] Pari etiam modo et Winilorum, hoc est Langobardorum, gens, quae postea in Italia feliciter regnavit, a Germanorum populis originem ducens, licet et aliae causae egressionis eorum asseverentur, ab insula quae Scadinavia dicitur adventavit.[3]

(Book I, c.1)

---

[1] The idea that the North teems with people, while those in the South sicken and die, is natural to Paul. His was an age swept by pandemic infections. These struck hardest in the temperate zones, and were less deadly in the northern and tropical zones. Germany should be seen as a factory of humanity only in the relative sense.

[2] The Rugii and Turcilingi were tribes first mentioned as inhabiting the shores of the Baltic. They were later found in the army of Attila and living close by the Danube. The Heroli were a migratory people appearing at different times in various parts of Europe. They were all among the troops of Odoacer, who conquered Italy in the fifth century.

[3] "Winelli" apparently means "eager for battle," or may be related to the Goth word "vinja," which means "pasture."

The Legend of the Seven Sleepers

Haud ab re esse arbitror, paulisper narrandi ordinem postponere, et quia adhuc stilus in Germania vertitur, miraculum, quod illic apud omnes celebre habetur, sed et quaedam alia, breviter intimare. In extremis circium versus Germaniae finibus, in ipso Oceani litore, antrum sub eminenti rupe conspicitur, ubi septem viri, incertum ex quo tempore, longo sopiti sopore quiescunt, ita inlaesis non solum corporibus, sed etiam vestimentis, ut ex hoc ipso, quod sine ulla per tot annorum curricula corruptione perdurant, apud indociles easdem et barbaras nationes veneratione habeantur. Hi denique, quantum ad habitum spectat, Romani esse cernuntur. E quibus dum unum quidam cupiditate stimulatus vellet exuere, mox eius, ut dicitur, brachia aruerunt, poenaque sua ceteros perterruit, ne quis eos ulterius contingere auderet. Videris, ad quod eos profectum per tot tempora providentia divina conservet. Fortasse horum quandoque, quia non aliter nisi Christiani esse putantur, gentes illae praedicatione salvandae sunt.[4]

(Book I, c.4)

The Scritobini and the Horrors of Barbarism Left Behind

Huic loco Scritobini, sic enim gens illa nominatur, vicini sunt. Qui etiam aestatis tempore nivibus non carent, nec aliud, utpote feris ipsis ratione non dispares, quam crudis agrestium animantium carnibus vescuntur; de quorum etiam hirtis pellibus sibi indumenta coaptant. Hi a saliendo iuxta linguam barbaram ethimologiam ducunt. Saltibus enim utentes, arte quadam ligno incurvo ad arcus similitudinem feras assequuntur. Apud hos est animal cervo non satis absimile, de cuius ego corio, ut fuerat pilis hispidum, vestem in modum tunicae genu tenus aptatam conspexi, sicut iam fati, ut relatum est, Scritobini, utuntur.

(Book I, c.5a)

---

[4] This is a version of the Story of the Seven Sleepers, which was very popular in late Antiquity and the Middle Ages. The earliest version we know is by Jacobus Sarugiensis, a Mesopotamian bishop. The story appears in Gregory of Tours, and in the Koran, where the Sleepers prophesy the coming of Mohammed. The common story, though, is that the Sleepers were young Christians in Ephesus. They withdrew into a cave in the reign of Decius, when the Pagans were persecuting the Christians, and woke from a miraculous sleep in the reign of Theodosius I over a hundred years later, when the Christians were persecuting each other. They were found out by their obsolete clothing, and by the money they tried to spend

Ancient Germany and the Roman Empire, c.200

On the Measurement of Latitude

Quibus in locis circa aestivale solstitium per aliquot dies etiam noctu clarissima lux cernitur, diesque ibi multo maiores quam alibi habentur; sicut e contrario circa brumale solstitium, quamvis diei lux adsit, sol tamen ibi non videtur, diesque minimi, quam usquam alibi, noctes quoque longiores existunt; quia scilicet, quanto magis a sole longius disceditur, tanto sol ipse terrae vicinior apparet et umbrae longiores excrescunt. Denique in Italia, sicut et antiqui scripserunt, circa diem Natalis Domini novem pedes in umbra staturae humanae hora sexta metiuntur. Ego autem in Gallia Belgica in loco qui Totonis villa dicitur constitutus, status mei umbram metiens, decem et novem et semis pedes inveni. Sic quoque contrario modo, quanto propinquius meridiem versus ad solem acceditur, tantum semper umbrae breviores videntur, in tantum ut solstitio aestivali, respiciente sole de medio caeli, in Aegypto et Hierosolimis et in eorum vicinitate constitutis locis nullae videantur umbrae. In Arabia vero hoc ipso tempore sol supra medium caeli ad partem aquilonis cernitur, umbraeque versa vice contra meridiem videntur.[5]

(Book I, c.5b)

---

[5] This passage alone is enough to prove that the Middle Ages were not sunk in barbarism and superstition. It shows that Paul has an experimental turn of mind, and is capable to forming hypotheses to explain his facts—and that he is able to extend his hypotheses to deduce other facts he has not observed.

Armed Men are Free Men

Igitur egressi de Scadinavia Winili, cum Ibor et Aione ducibus, in regionem quae appellatur Scoringa[6] venientes, per annos illic aliquot consederunt. Illo itaque tempore Ambri et Assi Wandalorum[7] duces vicinas quasque provincias bello premebant. Hi iam multis elati victoriis, nuntios ad Winilos mittunt, ut aut tributa Wandalis persolverent, aut se ad belli certamina praepararent. Tunc Ibor et Aio, adnitente matre Gambara, deliberant, melius esse armis libertatem tueri, quam tributorum eandem solutione foedare. Mandant per legatos Wandalis, pugnaturos se potius quam servituros. Erant siquidem tunc Winili universi iuvenili aetate florentes, sed numero perexigui, quippe qui unius non nimiae amplitudinis insulae tertia solummodo particula fuerint.

(Book I, c.7)

How the Lombards Got Their Name

Refert hoc loco antiquitas ridiculam fabulam: quod accedentes Wandali ad Godan[8] victoriam de Winilis postulaverint, illeque responderit, se illis victoriam daturum quos primum oriente sole conspexisset. Tunc accessisse Gambaram ad Fream, uxorem Godan, et Winilis victoriam postulasse, Freamque consilium dedisse, ut Winilorum mulieres solutos crines erga faciem ad barbae similitudinem componerent maneque primo cum viris adessent seseque a Godan videndas pariter e regione, qua ille per fenestram orientem versus erat solitus aspicere, collocarent. Atque ita factum fuisse. Quas cum Godan oriente sole conspiceret, dixisse: "Qui sunt isti longibarbi?." Tunc Fream subiunxisse, ut quibus nomen tribuerat victoriam condonaret. Sicque Winilis Godan victoriam concessisse. Haec risu digna sunt et pro nihilo habenda. Victoria enim non potestati est adtributa

---

[6] Scoringa—close by Hamburg.

[7] The Vandals were an East Germanic tribe who first appear in history inhabiting present-day southern Poland. Some of them were among the mass of barbarians who crossed the frozen Rhine in 406. In 409 they invaded Spain. In 429, under king Genseric (reigned 428-477), the Vandals entered North Africa. By 439 they established a kingdom which included the Roman province of Africa as well as Sicily, Corsica, Sardinia, Malta and the Balearic Islands. They fended off several Roman attempts to recapture the African province, and sacked the city of Rome in 455. Their kingdom collapsed in the Vandalic War of 533-34, in which Emperor Justinian I's forces managed to reconquer the Province for the Empire.

[8] "Godan"—otherwise Odin or Wotan.

hominum, sed de caelo potius ministratur.

Certum tamen est, Langobardos ab intactae ferro barbae longitudine, cum primitus Winili dicti fuerint, ita postmodum appellatos. Nam iuxta illorum linguam lang longam, bard barbam significat. Wotan sane, quem adiecta littera Godan dixerunt, ipse est qui apud Romanos Mercurius dicitur et ab universis Germaniae gentibus ut deus adoratur; qui non circa haec tempora, sed longe anterius, nec in Germania, sed in Grecia fuisse perhibetur.[9]

(Book I, c.8-9)

A Wicked Prostitute

His temporibus quaedam meretrix uno partu septem puerulos enixa, beluis omnibus mater crudelior in piscinam proiecit necandos. Hoc si cui impossibile videtur, relegat historias veterum, et inveniet, non solum septem infantulos, sed etiam novem unam mulierem semel peperisse. Et hoc certum est maxime apud Aegyptios fieri. Contigit itaque, ut rex Agelmund, dum iter carperet, ad eandem piscinam deveniret. Qui cum equo retento miserandos infantulos miraretur hastaque, quam manu gerebat, huc illucque eos inverteret, unus ex illis iniecta manu hastam regiam conprehendit. Rex misericordia motus factumque altius ammiratus, eum magnum futurum pronuntiat. Moxque eum a piscina levari praecepit, atque nutrici traditum omni cum studio mandat alendum; et quia eum de piscina, quae eorum lingua lama dicitur, abstulit, Lamissio eidem nomen inposuit. Qui cum adolevisset, tam strenuus iuvenis effectus est, ut et bellicosissimus extiterit et post Agelmundi funus regni gubernacula rexerit.

(Book I, c.15)

The Golden Age of Justinian: Conquests

Hac tempestate Iustinianus Augustus Romanum imperium felici sorte regebat.[10] Qui et bella prospere gessit et in causis civilibus mirificus extitit. Nam per Belisarium patricium Persas fortiter devicit, perque ipsum Belisarium Wandalorum gentem, capto eorum rege Gelismero, usque ad

---

[9] Modern scholars tend to disagree with Paul on how the Lombards got their names. "Bard" may not de derived from what became our word for "beard," but from "bord," from which we have "sea-board." On the other hand, Hodgekin (V,85) agrees with Paul.

[10] Justinian I (Emperor: 527–565); born 483, Tauresium, Dardania; died 565, Constantinople. Noted for his administrative reorganisation of the imperial government and for his sponsorship of a codification of laws known as the *Codex Justinianus* (534).

internicionem delevit Africamque totam post annos nonaginta et sex Romano imperio restituit. Rursumque Belisarii viribus Gothorum in Italia gentem, capto Witichis eorum rege, superavit. Mauros quoque post haec Africam infestantes eorumque regem Amtalan per Iohannem exconsulem mirabili virtute protrivit. Pari etiam modo et alias gentes belli iure conpressit. Quam ob causam propter horum omnium victorias, ut Alamannicus, Gothicus, Francicus, Germanicus, Anticus, Alanicus, Wandalicus Africanusque diceretur, habere agnomina meruit.

(Book I, c.25a)

The Golden Age of Justinian: Laws

Justinian

Leges quoque Romanorum, quarum prolixitas nimia erat et inutilis dissonantia, mirabili brevitate correxit. Nam omnes constitutiones principum, quae utique multis in voluminibus habebantur, intra duodecim libros coartavit idemque volumen Codicem Iustinianum appellari praecepit. Rursumque singulorum magistratuum sive iudicum leges, quae usque ad duo milia pene libros erant extensae, intra quinquaginta librorum numerum redegit, eumque Codicem Digestorum sive Pandectarum vocabulo nuncupavit. Quattuor etiam Institutionum libros, in quibus breviter universarum legum textus conprehenditur, noviter composuit. Novas quoque leges, quas ipse statuerat, in unum volumen redactas, eundem Codicem Novellarum nuncupari sancivit.

(Book I, c.25b)

The Golden Age of Justinian: The Hagia Sophia

Extruxit quoque idem princeps intra urbem Constantinopolim Christo domino, qui est sapientia Dei patris, templum, quod greco vocabulo Agian Sophian, id est sanctam sapientiam, nominavit. Cuius opus adeo cuncta aedificia excellit, ut in totis terrarum spatiis huic simile non possit inveniri. Erat enim hic princeps fide catholicus, in operibus rectus, in iudiciis iustus; ideoque ei omnia concurrebant in bonum.

(Book I, c.25c)

18

The Golden Age of Justinian: Learning

Huius temporibus Cassiodorus[11] apud urbem Romam tam seculari quam divina scientia claruit. Qui inter cetera quae nobiliter scripsit psalmorum praecipue occulta potentissime reseravit. Hic primitus consul, deinde senator, ad postremum vero monachus extitit. Hoc etiam tempore Dionisius[12] abba in urbe Roma constitutus paschale calculum miranda argumentatione composuit. Tunc quoque apud Constantinopolim Priscianus Caesariensis grammaticae artis, ut ita dixerim, profunda rimatus est.[13] Tuncque nihilominus Arator, Romanae Ecclesiae subdiaconus, poeta mirabilis, Apostolorum actus versibus exametris exaravit.[14]

(Book I, c.25d)

The Horrid Cup of Alboin

In eo proelio Alboin[15] Cunimundum occidit, caputque illius sublatum, ad bibendum ex eo poculum fecit. Quod genus poculi apud eos "scala" dicitur,

---

[11] Flavius Magnus Aurelius Cassiodorus Senator (c.480–c.575) exerted great influence on the preservation of works of classical literature in Christian monasteries from the sixth century through the Middle Ages. He is also an important source of information on the period of Ostrogothic rule in Italy.

[12] Dionysius Exiguus (c.470–c.544); a monk born in Scythia Minor (probably modern Bulgaria). He is best known as the inventor of the *Anno Domini* (AD) numbering system for years. Some churches adopted his *computus* (calculation) for the dates of Easter.

[13] Priscianus Caesariensis (fl. 500), commonly known as Priscian, was a Latin grammarian and the author of the *Institutes of Grammar* which was the standard textbook for the study of Latin during the Middle Ages. It also provided the raw material for the field of speculative grammar.

[14] Arator, of Liguria, a Christian poet, who lived during the sixth century. He was an orphan, and owed his early education to Laurentius, archbishop of Milan, and Ennodius, bishop of Pavia, who took great interest in him. After completing his studies, he practised with success as an advocate, and was appointed to an influential post at the court of Athalaric, king of the Ostrogoths. About 540, he left the service of the state, took orders and was elected sub-deacon of the Roman Church. He gained the favour of Pope Vigilius, to whom he dedicated his *De Actibus Apostolorum* (written about 544), which was much admired in the Middle Ages.

[15] Alboin (d. 572 or 573), King of the Lombards, and conqueror of Italy; succeeded his father Audoin about 565. The Lombards were at that time dwelling west of the Danube). In alliance with the Avars, an Asiatic people who had invaded Central Europe, Alboin defeated the Gepidae, a powerful nation on his eastern frontier, slew their king Cunimund, whose skull he fashioned into a drinking-cup, and whose daughter Rosamund he carried off and made his wife. More on this later in these extracts.

lingua vero Latina patera vocitatur.[16] Cuius filiam nomine Rosimundam cum magna simul multitudine diversi sexus et aetatis duxit captivam; quam, quia Chlotsuinda obierat, in suam, ut post patuit, perniciem, duxit uxorem.

(Book I, c.27)

The Lombards in Imperial Service

Igitur cum circumquaque frequentes Langobardorum victoriae personarent, Narsis[17] chartularius imperialis, qui tunc praeerat Italiae, bellum adversus Totilam Gothorum regem praeparans, cum iam pridem Langobardos foederatos haberet, legatos ad Alboin dirigit, quatenus ei pugnaturo cum Gothis auxilium ministraret. Tunc Alboin electam e suis manum direxit, qui Romanis adversus Getas suffragium ferrent. Qui per maris Adriatici sinum in. Italiam transvecti, sociati Romanis pugnam inierunt cum Gothis; quibus usque ad internicionem pariter cum Totila suo rege deletis, honorati multis muneribus victores ad propria remearunt. Omnique tempore quo Langobardi Pannoniam possederunt, Romanae rei publicae adversus aemulos adiutores fuerunt.

(Book II, c.1)

Narses and the Smack of Firm Government I

His temporibus Narsis etiam Buccellino duci bellum intulit. Quem Theudepertus rex Francorum, cum in Italiam introisset, reversus ad Gallias, cum Amingo alio duce ad subiciendam Italiam dereliquerat. Qui Buccellinus cum paene totam Italiam direptionibus vastaret et Theudeperto suo regi de praeda Italiae munera copiosa conferret, cum in Campania hiemare disponeret, tandem in loco cui Tannetum nomen est gravi bello a Narsete superatus, extinctus est. Amingus vero dum Windin Gothorum comiti contra

---

[16] The use of skull cups was common among nomadic peoples. It was a particular custom of the Avars, and that is from where the Lombards may have acquired it. Skull cups appear to have been part of a ritual, where drinking from the cup was a means of assuming the dead man's powers. If so, by drinking from his enemy's skull Alboin was taking his vital strength.

[17] Narses, (c. 480–574); general under Emperor Justinian I. A eunuch, Narses rose to be Grand Chamberlain and then Imperial Treasurer. Also a noted military commander, he was appointed, in 551, to direct operations against the Huns, Gepids, and Lombards, who were devastating the Balkans. Later that year, he was sent to finish the reconquest of Italy, taken by the Ostrogoths in the previous century. He achieved this with efficiency and economy, and remained there as civil and military ruler. In 567, Justinian's successor, Justin II, removed him from this command, and he retired to a villa near Naples. When the Lombards invaded Italy and conquered large parts of it the following year, it was rumoured that Narses had retaliated for his dismissal by inviting the Lombards into Italy. See later for this story.

Narsetem rebellanti auxilium ferre conatus fuisset, utrique a Narsete superati sunt. Windin captus Constantinopolim exiliatur. Amingus vero, qui ei auxilium praebuerat, Narsetis gladio perimitur. Tertius quoque Francorum dux nomine Leutharius, Buccellini germanus, dum multa praeda onustus ad patriam cuperet reverti, inter Veronam et Tridentum iuxta lacum Benacum propria morte defunctus est.

(Book II, c.2)

Narses and the Smack of Firm Government II

Habuit nihilominus Narsis certamen adversus Sinduald Brentorum regem, qui adhuc de Herulorum stirpe remanserat, quos secum in Italiam veniens olim Odoacar adduxerat. Huic Narsis fideliter sibi primum adhaerenti multa beneficia contulit; sed novissime superbe rebellantem et regnare cupientem, bello superatum et captum celsa de trabe suspendit. Eo quoque tempore Narsis patricius per Dagisteum magistrum militum, virum bellicosum et fortem, universos Italiae fines obtinuit. Hic Narsis prius quidem chartularius fuit, deinde propter virtutum merita patriciatus honorem promeruit. Erat autem vir piissimus, in religione catholicus, in pauperes munificus, in recuperandis basilicis satis studiosus, vigiliis et orationibus in tantum studens, ut plus supplicationibus ad Deum profusis quam armis bellicis victoriam obtineret.

(Book II, c.3)

The Great Plague

Huius temporibus in provincia praecipue Liguriae maxima pestilentia exorta est. Subito enim apparebant quaedam signacula per domos, ostia, vasa vel vestimenta, quae si quis voluisset abluere, magis magisque apparebant. Post annum vero expletum coeperunt nasci in inguinibus hominum vel in aliis deligatioribus locis glandulae in modum nucis seu dactuli, quas mox subsequebatur febrium intolerabilis aestus, ita ut in triduo homo extingueretur.[18] Sin vero aliquis triduum transegisset, habebat spem vivendi. Erant autem ubique luctus, ubique lacrimae. Nam, ut vulgi rumor habebat, fugientes cladem vitare, relinquebantur domus desertae habitatoribus, solis catulis domum servantibus. Peculia sola remanebant in pascuis, nullo adstante pastore. Cerneres pridem villas seu castra repleta agminibus hominum, postero vero die universis fugientibus cuncta esse in summo silentio. Fugiebant filii, cadavera insepulta parentum relinquentes, parentes obliti pietatis viscera natos relinquebant aestuantes. Si quem forte antiqua

---

[18] Perhaps Read "delicatioribilis" in place of "deligatioribus."

pietas perstringebat, ut vellet sepelire proximum, restabat ipse insepultus; et dum obsequebatur, perimebatur, dum funeri obsequium praebebat, ipsius funus sine obsequio manebat. Videres seculum in antiquum redactum silentium: nulla vox in rure, nullus pastorum sibilus, nullae insidiae bestiarum in pecudibus, nulla damna in domesticis volucribus. Sata transgressa metendi tempus intacta expectabant messorem; vinea amissis foliis radiantibus uvis inlaesa manebat hieme propinquante. Nocturnis seu diurnis horis personabat tuba bellantium, audiebatur a pluribus quasi murmur exercitus. Nulla erant vestigia commeantium, nullus cernebatur percussor, et tamen visus oculorum superabant cadavera mortuorum. Pastoralia loca versa fuerant in sepulturam hominum, et habitacula humana facta fuerant confugia bestiarum. Et haec quidem mala intra Italiam tantum usque ad fines gentium Alamannorum et Baioariorum solis Romanis acciderunt. [19]

(Book II, c.4)

Narses: Betrayed and Betrayer

Igitur deleta, ut dictum est, vel superata Narsis omni Gothorum gente, his quoque de quibus diximus pari modo devictis, dum multum auri sive argenti

---

[19] This is an account of the bubonic plague that first showed itself in Constantinople in 542, probably arriving on the grain ships from Egypt, to where it had probably come on trading ships from the East. Procopius claims that it killed ten thousand people there a day for ninety days. Since statistics before the Modern Age are more than usually works of the imagination, this may or may not be true. We are reasonably assured, however, that the plague spread along the trade routes to every part of the Mediterranean world and its economic dependencies, killing perhaps a third of the entire population. It may have destroyed the cultural hegemony the Greeks had enjoyed in Syria and Egypt since the time of Alexander the Great, and prepared these regions for swift conquest by the Arabs in the next century. It may have depopulated North Africa to the point where it ceased to be part of European Civilisation. It may have struck hard in the remains of Roman Britain, thereby enabling its final conquest by the Angles and Saxons. The plague returned about once every decade, until about 750, keeping populations in a downward cycle. One of its last main appearances was after the second siege of Constantinople by the Arabs in 717. This, plus the Slavic invasions, appears to have broken the continuity of Greece with its ancient past.

Paul's description of the plague may not be of any actual outbreak, but is a fair summary of the most terrible and far-reaching event of the early Middle Ages. All the cultural and economic and political changes between about 550 and 750 make sense only in the light of one of the two greatest pandemics in history.

For a classic discussion of the "Justinianic Plague," see: Jacques Le Goff and Jean-Nöel Biraben, "La peste dans de Haut Moyen Âge," *Annales. Économies, Sociétés, Civilisations*, 24 (6,), 1969, pp. 1484-1510.

seu ceterarum specierum divitias adquisisset, magnam a Romanis, pro quibus multa contra eorum hostes laboraverat, invidiam pertulit. Qui contra eum Iustiniano Augusto[20] et eius coniugi Sophiae in haec verba suggesserunt, dicentes quia expedierat Romanis Gothis potius servire quam Grecis, "ubi Narsis eunuchus imperat et nos servitio premit; et haec noster piissimus princeps ignorat. Aut libera nos de manu eius, aut certe et civitatem Romanam et nosmetipsos gentibus tradimus." Cumque hoc Narsis audisset, haec breviter retulit verba: "Si male feci Romanis, male inveniam." Tunc Augustus in tantum adversus Narsetem commotus est, ut statim in Italiam Longinum praefectum mitteret, qui Narsetis locum obtineret. Narsis vero, his cognitis, valde pertimuit; et in tantum maxime ab eadem Sophia Augusta territus est, ut regredi ultra Constantinopolim non auderet. Cui illa inter cetera, quia eunuchus erat, haec fertur mandasse, ut eum puellis in genicio lanarum faceret pensa dividere. Ad quae verba Narsis dicitur haec responsa dedisse: talem se eidem telam orditurum, qualem ipsa, dum viveret, deponere non possit. Itaque odio metuque exagitatus in Neapolim Campaniae civitatem secedens, legatos mox ad Langobardorum gentem dirigit, mandans, ut paupertina Pannoniae rura desererent et ad Italiam cunctis refertam divitiis possidendam venirent. Simulque multimoda pomorum genera aliarumque rerum species, quarum Italia ferax est, mittit, quatenus eorum ad veniendum animos possit inlicere. Langobardi laeta nuntia et quae ipsi praeoptabant gratanter suscipiunt deque futuris commodis animos adtollunt. Continuo apud Italiam terribilia noctu signa visa sunt, hoc est igneae acies in caelo apparuerunt, eum scilicet qui postea effusus est sanguinem coruscantes.[21]

(Book II, c.5)

Alboin Gathers His Forces

Alboin vero ad Italiam cum Langobardis profecturus ab amicis suis vetulis Saxonibus auxilium petit, quatenus spatiosam Italiam cum pluribus possessurus intraret. Ad quem Saxones plus quam viginti milia virorum cum uxoribus simul et parvulis, ut cum eo ad Italiam pergerent, iuxta eius voluntatem venerunt. Hoc audientes Chlotharius et Sigibertus, reges

---

[20] The year is 568. Read "Justino" for "Justiniano." It was Justin II who was the husband of Sophia and to whom this complaint was made.

[21] A good story, but probably not a true one. It is first told in the seventh century. Gregory of Tours, who lived at the time of the Lombard invasion, mentions the recall of Narses and the invasion, but not the betrayal. There is reason to believe that Narses died in Constantinople, and that the Emperor attended his funeral.

Francorum, Suavos aliasque gentes in locis de quibus idem Saxones exierant posuerunt.

(Book II, c.6)

A Deal with the Huns

Tunc Alboin sedes proprias, hoc est Pannoniam, amicis suis Hunnis contribuit, eo scilicet ordine, ut, si quo tempore Langobardis necesse esset reverti, sua rursus arva repeterent. Igitur Langobardi, relicta Pannonia, cum uxoribus et natis omnique supellectili Italiam properant possessuri. Habitaverunt autem in Pannonia annis quadraginta duobus. De qua egressi sunt mense aprili, per indictionem primam, alio die post sanctum Pascha, cuius festivitas eo anno iuxta calculi rationem ipsis kalendis aprilis fuit, cum iam a Domini incarnatione anni quingenti sexaginta octo essent evoluti.[22]

(Book II, c.7)

The Lombards Reach Their Promised Land

Igitur cum rex Alboin cum omni suo exercitu vulgique promiscui multitudine ad extremos Italiae fines pervenisset, montem qui in eisdem locis prominet ascendit, indeque, prout conspicere potuit, partem Italiae contemplatus est. Qui mons propter hanc, ut fertur, causam ex eo tempore mons Regis appellatus est. Ferunt, in hoc monte bisontes feras enutriri. Nec mirum, cum usque huc Pannonia pertingat, quae horum animantium ferax est. Denique retulit mihi quidam veracissimus senex, tale se corium in hoc monte occisi bisontis vidisse, in quo quindecim, ut aiebat, homines, unus iuxta alium potuissent cubare.

(Book II, c.8)

How Italy Got Its Name

Italia [...] ab Italo Siculorum duce, qui eam antiquitus invasit, nomen accepit. Sive ob hoc Italia dicitur, quia magni in ea boves, hoc est itali, habentur. Ab eo namque quod est italus per diminutionem, licet una littera

---

[22] The word "indictio" was fiscal in origin. When Constantine the Great reorganized the Empire, he established a fiscal cycle of fifteen years, beginning 313. Hence the word in chronology means the number attached to the year showing its place in a cycle of fifteen years. Usually, historians neglect to say *which* indiction they have in mind. Therefore, the addition of an *Anno Domini* date is of great help.

addita altera immutata vitulus, appellatur. Italia etiam Ausonia dicitur ab Ausono, Ulixis filio. Primitus tamen Beneventana regio hoc nomine appellata est; postea vero tota sic coepit Italia vocitari. Dicitur quoque etiam Latium Italia, pro eo quod Saturnus Iovem, suum filium, fugiens, intra eam invenisset latebram. Igitur postquam de Italiae provinciis vel ipsius nomine, intra quam res gestas describimus, sufficienter est dictum, nunc ad historiae ordinem redeamus.

(Book II, c.24)

The Fall of the Italian Cities

Alboin igitur Liguriam introiens, indictione ingrediente tertia, tertio nonas septembris, sub temporibus Honorati archiepiscopi Mediolanum[23] ingressus est.[24] Dehinc universas Liguriae civitates, praeter has quae in litore maris sunt positae, cepit. Honoratus vero archiepiscopus Mediolanum deserens, ad Genuensem urbem confugit. Paulus quoque patriarcha annos duodecim sacerdotium gerens, ab hac luce subtractus est regendamque ecclesiam Probino reliquit.

Ticinensis[25] eo tempore civitas ultra tres annos obsidionem perferens, se fortiter continuit, Langobardorum exercitu non procul iuxta eam ab occidentali parte residente. Interim Alboin, eiectis militibus, invasit omnia usque ad Tusciam, praeter Romam et Ravennam vel aliqua castra quae erant in maris litore constituta. Nec erat tunc virtus Romanis, ut resistere possint, quia et pestilentia, quae sub Narsete facta est, plurimos in Liguria et Venetiis extinxerat, et post annum, quem diximus fuisse ubertatis, fames nimia ingruens universam Italiam devastabat. Certum est autem, tunc Alboin multos secum ex diversis, quas vel alii reges vel ipse ceperat, gentibus ad Italiam adduxisse. Unde usque hodie eorum in quibus habitant vicos Gepidos, Vulgares, Sarmatas, Pannonios, Suavos, Noricos, sive aliis huiuscemodi nominibus appellamus.

(Book II, c.25-6)

---

[23] Mediolanum—Milan

[24] The year is 569. The nones fell on the 9th before the ides, both days being included, and the ides on upon the 15th March, May, July and October, and on the 13th of the remaining months. The nones therefore fell on the 7rh March, May, July and October and on the 5th of other months. The 3rd day before the nones of September, reckoned backward from. the 5th and including both days, would therefore be the 3rd September

[25] Ticinum—Pavia.

The Surrender of Pavia

At vero Ticinensis civitas post tres annos et aliquot menses obsidionem perferens, tandem se Alboin et Langobardis obsidentibus tradidit. In quam cum Alboin per portam quae dicitur Sancti Iohannis ab orientali urbis parte introiret, equus eius in portae medio concidens, quamvis calcaribus stimulatus, quamvis hinc inde hastarum verberibus caesus, non poterat elevari. Tunc unus ex eisdem Langobardis taliter regem adlocutus est dicens: "Memento, domine rex, quale votum vovisti. Frange tam durum votum, et ingredieris urbem. Vere etenim christianus est populus in hac civitate." Siquidem Alboin voverat quod universum populum, quia se tradere noluisset, gladio extingueret. Qui postquam tale votum disrumpens civibus indulgentiam promisit, mox eius equus consurgens, ipse civitatem ingressus, nulli laesionem inferens, in sua promissione permansit. Tunc ad eum omnis populus in palatium, quod quondam rex Theudericus construxerat, concurrens, post tantas miserias animum de spe iam fidus coepit futura relevare.

(Book II, c.27)

More on the Horrid Cup of Alboin

Qui rex postquam in Italia tres annos et sex menses regnavit, insidiis suae coniugis interemptus est.[26] Causa autem interfectionis eius fuit. Cum in convivio ultra quam oportuerat apud Veronam laetus resideret, cum poculo quod de capite Cunimundi regis sui soceri fecerat reginae ad bibendum vinum dari praecepit atque eam ut cum patre suo laetanter biberet invitavit. Hoc ne cui videatur impossibile, veritatem in Christo loquor; ego hoc poculum vidi in quodam die festo Ratchis principem ut illud convivis suis ostentaret manu tenentem. Igitur Rosemunda ubi rem animadvertit, altum concipiens in corde dolorem, quem conpescere non valens, mox in mariti necem patris funus vindicatura exarsit, consiliumque mox cum Helmichis, qui regis scilpor, hoc est armiger,[27] et conlactaneus erat, ut regem interficeret iniit.

(Book II, c.28a)

---

[26] The summer of 572 or 573.

[27] A good translation here might be "squire."

THE LAST BANQUET OF ALBOIN.

Sex and Blackmail

Qui reginae persuasit, ut ipsa Peredeo, qui erat vir fortissimus, in hoc consilium adsciret. Peredeo cum reginae suadenti tanti nefas consensum adhibere nollet, illa se noctu in lectulo suae vestiariae, cum qua Peredeo stupri consuetudinem habebat, supposuit; ubi Peredeo rem nescius veniens, cum regina concubuit.[28] Cumque illa patrato iam scelere ab eo quaereret, quam se esse extimaret, et ipse nomen suae amicae, quam esse putabat, nominasset, regina subiunxit: "Nequaquam ut putas, sed ego Rosemunda sum" inquit. "Certe nunc talem rem, Peredeo, perpetratam habes, ut aut tu Alboin interficies, aut ipse te suo gladio extinguet." Tunc ille intellexit malum quod fecit, et qui sponde noluerat, tali modo in regis necem coactus adsensit.

(Book II, c.28b)

---

[28] The lack of electric lighting explains much. Even so, would you unknowingly sleep with the wrong person? Perhaps the man was drunk at the time.

27

A Murder in the Royal Palace

Tunc Rosemunda, dum se Alboin in meridie sopori dedisset, magnum in palatio silentium fieri praecipiens, omnia alia arma subtrahens, spatam illius ad lectuli caput, ne tolli aut evaginari possit, fortiter conligavit, et, iuxta consilium Helmichis, Peredeo interfectorem omni bestia crudaior introduxit. Alboin subito de sopore experrectus, malum quod imminebat intellegens, manum citius ad spatam porrexit; quam strictius religatam abstrahere non valens, adprehenso tamen scabello subpedaneo, se cum eo per aliquod spatium defendit. Sed heu! pro dolor! vir bellicosissimus et summae audaciae nihil contra hostem praevalens, quasi unus de inertibus interfectus est, uniusque mulierculae consilio periit, qui per tot hostium strages bello famosissimus extitit. Cuius corpus cum maximo Langobardorum fletu et lamentis sub cuiusdam scalae ascensu, quae palatio erat contigua, sepultum est. Fuit autem statura procerus et ad bella peragenda toto corpore coaptatus. Huius tumulum nostris in diebus Giselpert, qui dux Veronensium fuerat, aperiens, spatam eius et si quid in ornatu ipsius inventum fuerat abstulit. Qui se ob hanc causam vanitate solita apud indoctos homines Alboin vidisse iactabat.

(Book II, c.28c)

The Rapacity and Punishment of an Emperor

Per haec tempora apud Constantinopolim, ut supra praemissum est, iustinus minor regnabat, vir in omni avaritia deditus, contemptor pauperum, senatorum spoliator.[29] Cui tanta fuit cupiditatis rabies, ut arcas iuberet ferreas fieri, in quibus ea quae rapiebat auri talenta congereret. Quem etiam ferunt in heresim Pelagianam dilapsum. Hic cum a divinis mandatis aurem cordis averteret, iusto Dei iudicio amisso rationis intellectu amens effectus est. Hic Tiberium Caesarem adscivit, qui eius palatium vel singulas provincias gubernaret, hominem iustum, utilem, strenuum, sapientem, elemosinarium, in iudiciis aequum, in victoriis clarum et, quod his omnibus supereminet, verissimum christianum. Hic cum multa de thesauris quos Iustinus adgregaverat pauperibus erogaret, Sophia Augusta frequentius eum increpabat, quod rem publicam redigisset in paupertatem, dicens: "Quod ego

---

[29] Justin II (Emperor: 565–578); nephew of Justinian I, and husband of Sophia, the niece of the late empress Theodora. After inheriting an expanded empire from his uncle, Justinian I, Justin II's refusal to pay bribes to his potential enemies as his uncle had resulted in increased warfare along the extended borders of the empire. In his reign, much of Italy fell to the Lombards. His last four years were beset by a growing insanity and the passing of power to his wife Sophia and Tiberius, his successor.

multis annis congregavi, tu infra paucum tempus prodige dispergis." Agebat autem ille: "Confido in Domino, quia non deerit pecunia fisco nostro, tantum ut pauperes elemosinam accipiant aut captivi redimantur. Hoc est enim magnum thesaurum, dicente Domino: "Thesaurizate vobis thesauros in caelo, ubi neque aerugo neque tinea corrumpit, et ubi fures non effodiunt nec furantur."[30] Ergo de his quae Dominus tribuit congregemus thesauros in caelo et Dominus nobis augere dignabitur in saeculo." Igitur Iustinus cum undecim annis regnasset, amentiam, quam incurrerat, tandem cum vita finivit. Bella sane, quae per Narsetem patricium Gothis vel Francis inlata superius per anticipationem diximus, huius temporibus gesta sunt. Denique et cum Roma temporibus Benedicti papae, vastantibus omnia per circuitum Langobardis, famis penuria laboraret, multa milia frumenti navibus ab Aegypto dirigens, eam suae studio misericordiae relevavit.

(Book III, c.11)

The Generosity of an Emperor

Mortuo igitur Iustino, Tiberius Constantinus, Romanorum regum quinquagesimus, sumpsit imperium.[31] Hic cum, ut superius diximus, sub Iustino adhuc Caesar palatium regeret et multas cottidie elemosinas faceret, magnam ei Dominus auri copiam subministravit. Nam deambulans per palatium vidit in pavimento domus tabulam marmoream, in qua erat crux dominica sculpta, et ait: "Crucem Domini frontem nostram et pectora munire debemus, et ecce eam sub pedibus conculcamus." Et dicto citius iussit eandem tabulam auferri. Defossamque tabulam atque erectam, inveniunt subter et aliam hoc Signum habentem. Qui et ipsam iussit auferri. Qua amota, repperiunt et tertiam. Iussuque eius cum et haec fuisset ablata, inveniunt magnum thesaurum habentem supra mille auri centenaria. Sublatumque aurum, pauperibus adhuc abundantius quam consueverat largitur. Narsis quoque patricius Italiae cum in quadam civitate intra Italiam domum magnam haberet, cum multis thesauris ad supra memoratam urbem advenit; ibique in domo sua occulte cisternam magnam fodit, in qua multa milia centenariorum auri argentique reposuit. Interfectisque omnibus

---

[30] Matt 6:20

[31] Tiberius II (Emperor: 574–582). He took control of the Empire when Justin II went mad. He took advantage of peace with the Persians to try restoring Imperial power in the West. He made peace with the Visigoths in Spain and defeated the Berbers in North Africa. Meanwhile, the Slavs began to migrate into the Balkans in 579. Tiberius was now preoccupied by renewed war with Persia, and was unable to stop the Slavic migrations. In 582, Tiberius fell ill, and Maurice was named his heir. Maurice became emperor when Tiberius died in August 574, by poison, it was rumoured.

consciis, uni tantummodo seni haec per iuramentum ab eo exigens commendavit. Defuncto vero Narsete, supradictus senex ad Caesarem Tiberium veniens, dixit: "Si" inquit "mihi aliquid prodest, magnam rem tibi, Caesar, edicam." Cui ille: "Dic" ait "quod vis; proderitenim tibi, si quid nobis profuturum esse narraveris." "Thesaurum" inquit "Narsetis reconditum habeo quod in extremo vitae positus celare non possum." Tunc Caesar Tiberius gavisus mittit usque ad locum pueros suos. Recedente vero sene hi secuntur attoniti; pervenientesque ad cisternam, deopertamque ingrediuntur. In qua tantum aurum vel argentum repertum est, ut per multos dies vix a deportantibus potuisset evacuari. Quae ille paene omnia secundum suum morem erogatione largiflua dispensavit egenis.

(Book III, c.12)

Map of Italy at the Death of Alboin, 572

The Lombards in Italy: Wise and Benificent Rulers

At vero Langobardi cum per annos decem sub potestate ducum fuissent, tandem communi consilio Authari, Clephonis filium supra memorati principis, regem sibi statuerunt. Quem etiam ob dignitatem Flavium appellarunt.[32] Quo praenomine omnes qui postea fuerunt Langobardorum reges feliciter usi sunt. Huius in diebus ob restaurationem regni duces qui tunc erant omnem substantiarum suarum medietatem regalibus usibus tribuunt, ut esse possit, unde rex ipse sive qui ei adhaererent eiusque obsequiis per diversa officia dediti alerentur. Populi tamen adgravati per Langobardos hospites partiuntur.[33] Erat sane hoc mirabile in regno Langobardorum: nulla erat violentia, nullae struebantur insidiae; nemo aliquem iniuste angariabat, nemo spoliabat; non erant furta, non latrocinia; unusquisque quo libebat securus sine timore pergebat.

(Book III, c.16)

Floods in Italy

Eo tempore fuit aquae diluvium in finibus Venetiarum et Liguriae seu ceteris regionibus Italiae, quale post Noe tempore creditur non fuisse. Factae sunt lavinae possessionum seu villarum, hominumque pariter et animan tium magnus interitus. Destructa sunt itinera, dissipatae viae, tantumtuncque Atesis fluvius excrevit, ut circa basilicam Beati Zenonis martyris, quae extra Veronensis urbis muros sita est, usque ad superiores fenestras aqua per tingeret, licet, sicut et beatus Gregorius post papa scripsit, in eandem basilicam aqua minime introierit. Urbis quoque eiusdem Veronensis muri ex parte aliqua eadem sunt inundatione subruti. Facta est autem haec inundatio sexto decimo kalendas novembris. Sed tantae coruscationes et tonitrua fuerunt, quantae fieri vix aestivo tempore solent. Post duos quoque menses eadem urbs Veronen sium magna ex parte incendio concremata est.

(Book III, c.23)

---

[32] A title borrowed from the family name of Vespasian and Titus, afterwards used by a number of their successors, and also claimed by other rulers—for example, the Visigothic kings of Spain after Recared. Its use by Authari may be taken as the beginning of acceptance by the Italian people of the new order of things, and of the growing assimilation of the Lombards to Roman ways.

[33] "Populi tamen adgravati per Langobardos hospites partiunter." This is one of the most important statements in Paul, as it gives us nearly all we have on the condition of Italy in the early Lombard Period. Sadly, no one agrees what it means. It may be that the Italians were oppressed by their new lords. Or, given the flourishing state of Italy, and the use of "Flavius" as a legitimising title, things may have been better between the invaders and their subjects.

Plague in Rome

In hac diluvii effusione in tantum apud urbem Romam fluvius Tiberis excrevit, ut aquae eius super muros urbis influerent et maximas in ea regiones occuparent. Tunc per alveum eiusdem fluminis cum multa serpentium multitudine draco etiam mirae magnitudinis per urbem transiens usque ad mare discendit. Subsecuta statim est hanc inundationem gravissima pestilentia, quam inguinariam appellant.[34] Quae tanta strage populum devastavit, ut de inaestimabili multitudine vix pauci remanerent. Primumque Pelagium papam, virum venerabilem, perculit et sine mora extinxit. Deinde, pastore interempto, sese per populos extendit.

(Book III, c.24a)

Pope Gregory the Great

In hac tanta tribulatione beatissimus Gregorius, qui tunc levita erat, a cunctis generaliter papa electus est.[35] Qui dum septiformem laetaniam fieri ordinasset, intra unius horae spatium, dum hi Deum deprecarentur, octuaginta ex eis subito ad terram corruentes, spiritum exalarunt. Septiformis autem laetania ideo dicta est, quia omnis urbis populus a beato Gregorio in septem partes deprecaturus Dominum est divisus. In primo namque choro fuit omnis clerus, in secundo omnes abbates cum monachis suis, in tertio omnes abbatissae cum congregationibus suis, in quarto omnes infantes, in quinto omnes laici, in sexto universae viduae, in septimo omnes mulieres coniugatae. Ideo autem de beato Gregorio plura dicere obmittimus, quia iam ante aliquot annos eius vitam, Deo auxiliante, teximus. In qua quae dicenda fuerant iuxta tenuitatis nostrae vires universa descripsimus.

(Book III, c.24b)

Drought in Italy and Sundry Portents

Hoc anno fuit siccitas nimium gravis a mense ianuario usque ad mensem septembrium; et facta est magna penuria famis. Venit quoque et magna locustarum multitudo in territorium Tridentinum, quae maiores erant quam

---

[34] Another outbreak of the bubonic plague?

[35] Gregory the Great (Pope: 590– 604); the son of a Senator; famous for sending the first proper mission from Rome to convert the Anglo-Saxon barbarians in England. A ruler of great talent, he successfully established Papal supremacy in the West, bringing the rulers of France and Spain from the Arian heresy to Catholicism. This alignment did much to shape the future of Mediaeval Europe.

ceterae locustae; et mirum dictu, herbas paludesque depastae sunt, segetes vero agrorum exigue contigerunt. Sequenti quoque anno pari nihilominus modo adventarunt....

Inter haec sequenti mense ianuario paruit stella cometes mane et vespere per totum mensem. Eo quoque mense defunctus est Iohannes archiepiscopus Ravennae. Cuius in locum Marianus civis Romanus substitutus est. Evin quoque duce in Tridentu mortuo, datus est eidem loco dux Gaidoaldus, vir bonus ac fide catholicus. Isdem ipsis diebus Baioarii usque ad duo milia virorum dum super Sclavos inruunt, superveniente Cacano omnes interficiuntur. Tunc primum cavalli silvatici et bubali in Italiam delati, Italiae populis miracula fuerunt.

Subsequenti tempore rursum Ravennam et eos qui circa ora maris erant pestis gravissima vastavit. Sequenti quoque anno mortalitas valida populos Veronensium attrivit.

Tunc etiam signum sanguineum in caelo apparuisse visum est et quasi hastae sanguineae et lux clarissima per totam noctem. Theudepertus rex Francorum eo tempore cum Clothario patruele suo bellum gerens, eius exercitum vehementer adflixit.

(Book IV, c.2,10,14.16)

Diplomatic Relations with the Empire and Lombard Fashions

Hac etiam tempestate misit rex Agilulf Stablicianum notarium suum Constantinopolim ad Focatem imperatorem. Qui rediens cum legatis imperatoris, facta pace annuali, Agilulfo regi idem legati imperialia munera optulere.[36]

[In Modicia Theudelinda regina] sibi palatium condidit, in quo aliquid et de Langobardorum gestis depingi fecit. In qua pictura manifeste ostenditur, quomodo Langobardi eo tempore comam capitis tondebant, vel qualis illis vestitus qualisve habitus erat. Siquidem cervicem usque ad occipitium radentes nudabant, capillos a facie usque ad os dimissos habentes, quos in utramque partem in frontis discrimine dividebant. Vestimenta vero eis erant laxa et maxime linea, qualia Anglisaxones[37] habere solent, ornata institis

---

[36] The first record of direct negotiations between the Lombards and the Empire. It seems increasingly to have been felt on all sides that the Lombards were in Italy to stay.

[37] Apparently the first written mention of the Anglo-Saxons.

latioribus vario colore contextis. Calcei vero eis erant usque ad summum pollicem pene aperti et alternatim laqueis corrigiarum retenti. Postea vero coeperunt osis uti, super quas equitantes tubrugos birreos mittebant. Sed hoc de Romanorum consuetudine traxerant.

(Book IV, c.35, 22)

The Tyranny of Phocas and the Pantheon

Focas[38] igitur, ut praemissum est, extincto Mauricio eiusque filius,[39] Romanorum regnum invadens, per octo annorum curricula principatus est. Hic rogante papa Bonifacio statuit sedem Romanae et apostolicae ecclesiae caput esse omnium ecclesiarum, quia ecclesia Constantinopolitana prima se omnium ecclesiarum scribebat.[40] Idem alio papa Bonifacio petente iussit, in veteri fano quod Pantheum vocabatur, ablatis idolatriae sordibus, ecclesiam beatae semper virginis Mariae et omnium martyrum fieri, ut, ubi quondam omnium non deorum, sed demoniorum cultus agebatur, ibi deinceps omnium fieret memoria sanctorum.[41] Huius tempore Prasini et Veneti per orientem et Aegyptum civile bellum faciunt ac sese mutua caede prosternunt.[42] Persae

---

[38] "Focas"—"Phocas" (Emperor: 602–610); came to power in a revolt against Emperor Maurice. Phocas captured Constantinople and overthrew Maurice on the 23rd November 602, declaring himself Emperor on the same day. He distrusted the ruling *elite*, and installed his relatives in high military positions, and purged his opponents. Phocas was an incompetent leader, both of the administration and army, and under him the Empire was threatened by multiple enemies, with frequent raids in the Balkans from the Avars and Slavs, and a Persian invasion of the Eastern Provinces. Because of his incompetence and brutality, the Exarch of Carthage, Heraclius the Elder, rebelled against him. His son, Heraclius the Younger, took Constantinople on the 5th October 610, and executed Phocas on the same day, before declaring himself Emperor. For further information, see: Richard Blake, *Terror of Constantinople*, Hodder & Stoughton, London, 2009.

[39] For "filius," read "fillii."

[40] It was Phocas who first gave the Pope the title of Universal Bishop. For this reason, the Popes of the day overlooked his many crimes within the Empire.

[41] The Pantheon was consecrated as the Church of St. Mary and the Martyrs on the 13th May 609. Built by Agrippa in the time of Augustus, and remodelled by Hadrian, it is the only substantial ancient building which has fully survived. An account of Rome in 609 is given in: Richard Blake, *Conspiracies of Rome*, Hodder & Stoughton, London, 2008.

[42] A reference here, that Paul may not himself understand, to the Hippodrome riots in Constantinople between the Greens and the Blues. The Circus Factions were rather like our own football supporters—but with deadly force and often a political agenda. In the previous century, these factions had twice reduced the Imperial City to chaos.

quoque adversus rem publicam gravissima bella gerentes, multas Romanorum provincias et ipsam Hierusolimam auferunt.[43] Et destruentes ecclesias, sancta quoque profanantes, inter ornamenta locorum sanctorum vel communium etiam vexillum dominicae crucis abducunt. Contra hunc Focatem Eraclianus, qui Africam regebat, rebellavit, atque cum exercitu veniens, eum regno vitaque privavit remque publicam Romanam Eraclius, eiusdem filius, regendam suscepit.[44]

(Book IV, c.36)

The Avars Invade Italy

Circa haec tempora rex Avarum, quem sua lingua Cacanum appellant, cum innumerabili multitudine veniens, Venetiarum fines ingressus est.[45] Huic Gisulfus Foroiulanus[46] dux cum Langobardis, quos habere poterat, audacter occurrit; sed quamvis forti animositate contra inmensam multitudinem bellum cum paucis gereret, undique tamen circumseptus, cum omnibus pene suis extinctus est. Uxor vero eiusdem Gisulfi nomine Romilda cum Langobardis qui evaserant sive eorum uxoribus et filiis qui in bello perierant, intra murorum Foroiulani castri se muniit septa. Huic erant filii Taso et

---

[43] A slip of chronology here. Jerusalem was not lost to the Persians until 614, during the reign of Heraclius, who was Emperor after Phocas. It was then that the True Cross was carried off into a captivity that lasted until the great offensive that Heraclius mounted in the 620s, when he took back all the Persians had taken since 602, and indeed shattered the Persian Empire.

[44] Heraclius (Emperor: 610–641); took power in a rebellion and civil war from Phocas; introduced Greek as the Empire's official language, rather than Latin. His reign can be summarised as: catastrophe, triumph, catastrophe. When he took power, the Empire was threatened on every frontier the most critical being in the East, where the Persians were reviving the empire of Cyrus and Xerxes. Within ten years, however, Hercalius had reformed the civil and military administration of the Empire, and was able, in a series of campaigns, to retake all the lost territory and to destroy Persia as a great power. He was unprepared for the Islamic explosion of 634. In that year, the Arabs took Persia in a single campaign. They soon overran Mesopotamia, Armenia and Egypt. For the next hundred years, the Empire was on the defensive—a fact useful to the Lombards.

[45] The date usually given is 611. Until this time, the Lombards and the Avars had enjoyed friendly relations. But the Avars appear to have been a most vicious race of barbarians— unlike the Lombards in showing no capacity for civilisation. They devastated the Balkans, burning as far south as Corinth. They had similar ambitions for Italy. The purpose of this whole chapter, I think, lies in Paul's desire to show his own people as true Italian patriots, defending their new country against a much greater menace than they had been, and were. It is also to show the heroism of young Grimoald, and allows Paul to speak of his own ancestry.

[46] Foroiulanus—Friuli

Cacco iam adulescentes, Raduald vero et Grimuald adhuc in puerili aetate constituti. Habebat vero et filias quattuor, quarum una Appa, alia Gaila vocabatur, duarum vero nomina non retinemus. Communierant se quoque Langobardi et in reliquis castris quae his vicina erant, hoc est in Cormones, Nemas, Osopo, Artenia, Reunia, Glemona, vel etiam in Ibligine,[47] cuius positio omnino inexpugnabilis existit. Pari etiam modo et in reliquis castellis, ne Hunnis, hoc est Avaribus, praeda fierent, se communivere. Avares vero per omnes Foroiulanorum fines discurrentes, omnia incendiis et rapinis vastantes, Foroiulanum oppidum obsidione claudunt et totis viribus expugnare moliuntur.

(Book IV, c.37a)

The Avars and a Treacherous Queen

Horum rex, id est Cacanus, dum circa muros armatus cum magno equitatu perambularet, ut, qua ex parte urbem facilius expugnare posset, inquireret, hunc Romilda de muris prospiciens, cum eum cerneret iuvenili aetate florentem, meretrix nefaria concupivit, eique mox per nuntium mandavit, ut, si eam in matrimonium sumeret, ipsa eidem civitatem cum omnibus qui aderant traderet. Quod rex barbarus audiens, eidem malignitatis dolo quod mandaverat se facturum promisit eamque se in matrimonium accipere spopondit. Illa vero nihil morata, portas Foroiulensis castri aperuit et ad suam cunctorumque qui aderant perniciem hostem introduxit. Ingressi vero Avares cum rege suo Forumiulii, universa quae invenire poterant rapinis diripiunt; ipsamque urbem flammis concremantes, universos quos reppererant captivos adducunt,[48] fallaciter tamen, eis promittentes, quod eos, unde digressi fuerant, Pannoniae in finibus conlocarent. Qui cum patriam revertentes ad campum quem Sacrum nominant pervenissent, omnes qui iam in maiori aetate constituti erant Langobardos gladio perimere statuunt, mulieres vero et parvulos captivitatis sorte dividunt.

(Book IV, c.37b)

The Heroism of Young Grimoald

Taso vero et Cacco seu Raduald, filii Gisulfi et Romildae, cum hanc Avarorum malitiam cognovissent, statim ascensis equis fugam arripiunt. E quibus unus Grimoaldum puerulum fratrem suum, dum existimaret utpote

---

[47] Modern names: Cormons, Artegna, Ragogna, Gemona, Iplis.

[48] For "adducunt," read "abducunt."

parvulum super equum currentem se tenere non posse, melius ducens eundem gladio perimere quam captivitatis iugum sustinere, eum occidere voluit. Cum igitur ut eum percuteret lanceam elevasset, puer lacrimans exclamavit, dicens: "Noli me pungere, quia possum me super equum tenere." Qui iniecta manu eum per brachium adprehendens super nudum equi dorsum posuit eundemque ut si posset se continere hortatus est. Puer vero frenum equi manu arripiens, fugientes germanos et ipse secutus est. Quo conperto, Avares mox ascensis equis eos persecuti sunt; sed reliquis veloci fuga evadentibus, Grimoald puerulus ab uno eorum, qui velocius cucurrerat, capitur.[49] Nec tamen eum suus conprehensor gladio ferire propter parvitatem aetatis dignatus est, sed sibi eundem potius serviturum reservavit. Cumque eum ad castra revertens adprehenso eiusdem equi freno reduceret deque tam nobili praeda exultaret erat enim ipse puerulus eleganti forma, micantibus oculis, lacteo crine perfusus; qui cum se captivum trahi doleret,

Ingentes animos angusto in pectore versans,[50]

ensem, qualem in illa aetate habere poterat, vagina exemit seque trahentem Avarem, quantulo adnisu valuit, capitis in verticem percussit. Moxque ad cerebrum ictus perveniens, hostis ab equo deiectus est.[51] Puer vero Grimuald verso equo fugam laetabundus arripiens, tandem fratribus iunctus est eisque liberatione sua, nuntiato insuper hostis interitu, inaestimabile gaudium fecit. Avares vero omnes Langobardos qui iam in virili aetate erant gladio perimunt, mulieres vero et parvulos captivitatis iugo addicunt.

(Book IV, c.37c)

Gang-Rape and Rotten Meat

Romildam vero, quae totius malitiae caput extitit, rex Avarum propter iusiurandum, sicut ei spoponderat, nocte una quasi in matrimonio habuit, novissime vero duodecim Avaribus tradidit, qui eam per totam noctem

---

[49] Grimoald I (King of the Lombards: 662–671). Born before 610 to Duke Gisulf II of Friuli and the Bavarian princess Romilda, daughter of Duke Garibald I of Bavaria, and as such descended from the Gausian Dynasty of the first Lombard kings in Italy. He succeeded his brother Radoald in 646/7 as duke of Benevento. His greatness as a military leader saved the Lombard Kingdom from the attempted reconquest by Constans II. See subsequent passages for this history.

[50] Vergil, *Georgics*, IV, 83—"versant" is changed here to "versans."

[51] The meaning of this should be clear, but note the use of the nominative here, instead of the ablative.

vicibus sibi succedentes libidine vexarent. Postmodum quoque palum in medio campo configi praecipiens, eandem in eius acumine inseri mandavit, haec insuper exprobrando inquiens: "Talem te dignum est maritum habere." Igitur dira proditrix patriae tali exitio periit, quae amplius suae libidini quam civium et consanguineorum saluti prospexit. Filiae vero eius non matris libidinem secutae, sed castitatis amore studentes ne a barbaris contaminarentur, crudorum pullorum carnes sibi inter mammas sub fascia posuerunt, quae ex calore putrefactae odorem foetidum exalabant. Cumque eas vellent Avares contingere, non sustinentes foetorem, putabant eas naturaliter ita foetere, procul ab eis cum execratione recedentes atque dicentes, omnes Langobardas foetidas esse. Hac igitur arte Avarorum libidinem puellae nobiles evadentes, et ipsae castae servatae sunt et utile servandae castitatis, si quid tale feminis contigerit, mandaverunt exemplum. Quae postea per diversas regiones venundatae, iuxta nobilitatem suam dignis sunt nuptiis potitae. Nam una earum Alamannorum regi, alia vero dicitur Baioariorum principi nupsisse.

(Book IV, c.37d)

Paul's Family History I

Exigit vero nunc locus, postposita generali historia, pauca etiam privatim de mea, qui haec scribo, genealogia retexere, et quia res ita postulat, paulo superius narrationis ordinem replicare. Eo denique tempore quo Langobardorum gens de Pannoniis ad Italiam venit, Leupchis meus abavus ex eodem Langobardorum genere cum eis pariter adventavit. Qui postquam aliquot annos in Italia vixit, diem claudens extremum, quinque ex se genitos filios adhuc parvulos reliquit; quos tempestas ista captivitatis, de qua nunc diximus, conprehendens, omnes ex castro Foroiulensi in Avarorum patriam exules deduxit. Qui cum per multos annos in eadem regione captivitatis miseriam sustinuissent et iam ad virilem pervenissent aetatem, ceteris quattuor, quorum nomina non retinemus, in captivitatis angustia persistentibus, quintus eorum germanus nomine Lopichis, qui noster postea proavus extitit, inspirante sibi, ut credimus, misericordiae auctore, captivitatis iugum abicere statuit et ad Italiam, quo gentem Langobardorum residere meminerat, tendere atque ad libertatis iura studuit reppedare.

(Book IV, c.37e)

Paul's Family History II

Qui cum adgressus fugam adripuisset, faretram tantum et arcum et aliquantulum cibi propter viaticum gerens, nesciretque omnino quo pergeret, ei lupus adveniens comes itineris et ductor effectus est. Qui cum ante eum pergeret et frequenter post se respiceret et cum stante subsisteret atque cum pergente praeiret, intellexit, sibi eum divinitus datum esse, ut ei iter, quod nesciebat, ostenderet. Cum per aliquot dies per montium solitudines hoc modo pergerent, panis eidem viatori, quem exiguum habuerat, omnino defecit. Qui cum ieiunans iter carperet et iam fame tabefactus defecisset, tetendit arcum suum et eundem lupum, ut eum in cibum sumere possit, sagitta interficere voluit. Sed lupus idem ictum ferientis praecavens, sic ab eius visione elapsus est. Ipse autem, recedente eodem lupo, nesciens quo pergeret, insuper famis penuria nimium debilis effectus, cum iam de vita desperaret, sese in terram proiciens, obdormivit; viditque quendam virum in somnis talia sibi verba dicentem: "Surge! Quid dormis? Arripe viam in hanc partem contra quam pedes tenes; illac etenim est Italia, ad quam tendis." Qui statim surgens, in illam partem quam in somnis audierat pergere coepit; nec mora, ad habitaculum hominum pervenit. Erat enim Sclavorum habitatio in illis locis. Quem cum una mulier iam vetula vidisset, statim intellexit, eum fugitivum esse et famis penuria laborare. Ducta autem misericordia super eum, abscondit eum in domo sua et secreto paulatim ei victum ministravit, ne, si ei usque ad saturitatem alimoniam praeberet, eius vitam funditus extingueret. Denique sic conpetenter ei pastum praebuit, quousque ipse recuperatus vires accipere potuisset. Cumque eum iam validum ad iter faciendum vidisset, datis ei cibariis, ad quam partem tendere deberet, admonuit.

(Book IV, c.37f)

Paul's Family History III

Qui post aliquot dies Italiam ingressus, ad domum in qua ortus fuerat pervenit; quae ita deserta erat, ut non solum tectum non haberet, sed etiam rubis et sentibus plena esset. Quibus ille succisis intra eosdem parietes vastam hornum repperiens, in ea suam faretram suspendit. Qui postea consanguineorum et amicorum suorum muneribus dotatus, et domum reaedificavit et uxorem duxit; sed nihil de rebus quas genitor suus habuerat, exclusus iam ab his qui eas invaserant longa et diuturna possessione, conquirere potuit. Iste, ut iam superius praemisi, extitit meus proavus. Hic etenim genuit avum meum Arichis, Arichis vero patrem meum Warnefrit, Warnefrit autem ex Theudelinda coniuge genuit me Paulum meumque germanum Arichis, qui nostrum avum. cognomine retulit. Haec paucis de propriae genealogiae serie delibatis, nunc generalis historiae revertamur ad tramitem.

(Book IV, c.37g)

The Empire Strikes Back

His diebus Constantinus Augustus,[52] qui et Constans est appellatus, Italiam a Langobardorum manu eruere cupiens, Constantinopoli egressus, per litoralia iter habens, Athenas venit, indeque mare transgressus, Tarentum applicuit.[53] Qui tamen prius ad solitarium quendam, qui prophetiae spiritum habere dicebatur, adiit, studiose ab eo sciscitans, utrum gentem Langobardorum, quae in Italia habitabat, superare et optinere possit. A quo cum servus Dei spatium unius noctis expetisset, ut pro hoc ipso Dominum supplicaret, facto mane ita eidem Augusto respondit: "Gens Langobardorum superari modo ab aliquo non potest, quia regina quaedam ex alia provincia veniens basilicam beati Iohannis baptistae in Langobardorum finibus construxit, et propter hoc ipse beatus Iohannes pro Langobardorum gente continue intercedit. Veniet autem tempus, quando ipsum oraculum habebitur despectui, et tunc gens ipsa peribit." Quod nos ita factum esse probavimus, qui ante Langobardorum perditionem eandem beati Iohannis basilicam, quae utique in loco qui Modicia dicitur est constituta, per viles personas ordinari conspeximus, ita ut indignis et adulteris non pro vitae merito, sed praemiorum datione, isdem locus venerabilis largiretur.

(Book V, c.6)

---

[52] Constans II (Emperor: 642–668). Born 631, and became Emperor, when only eleven, on the death of his father, Constantine III. During his reign the Arabs continued their conquest of the non-Greek areas of the Empire. In 663, he arrived in Italy, to reconquer it for the Empire. He launched an assault against the Lombard Duchy of Benevento, which then included most of Southern Italy. Taking advantage of the fact that Lombard King Grimoald I was at war with the Franks, Constans disembarked at Taranto and besieged Lucera and Benevento. However, the latter resisted and Constans withdrew to Naples. During the journey from Benevento to Naples, He was defeated by Mitolas, Count of Capua, near Pugna. Constans ordered Saburrus, the commander of his army, again to attack the Lombards, but he was defeated by the Beneventani at Forino, between Avellino and Salerno. In 663 Constans visited Rome for twelve days—the first emperor to set foot in Rome for two centuries—and was received with great honour by Pope Vitalian (657–672). Although on friendly terms with Vitalian, he stripped buildings, including the Pantheon, of their ornaments and bronze to be carried back to Constantinople, and in 666 declared the Pope to have no jurisdiction over the Archbishop of Ravenna, since that city was the seat of the Exarch, his immediate representative. His subsequent moves in Calabria and Sardinia were marked by further strippings and demands for taxes that enraged his Italian subjects. At last, he settled in Syracuse, where, on the 15th September 668, he was assassinated in his bath.

[53] 662

The Mediterranean World, c.650

The Lombards: Expulsion from Italy?

Igitur cum, ut diximus, Constans Augustus Tarentum venisset, egressus exinde, Beneventanorum fines invasit omnesque pene per quas venerat Langobardorum civitates cepit. Luceriam quoque, opulentam Apuliae civitatem, expugnatam fortius invadens diruit, ad solum usque prostravit. Agerentia[54] sane propter munitissimam loci positionem capere minime potuit. Deinde cum omni suo exercitu Beneventum circumdedit et eam vehementer expugnare coepit; ubi tunc Rumuald, Grimualdi filius adhuc iuvenulus,[55] ducatum tenebat. Qui statim ut imperatoris adventum cognovit, nutricium suum nomine Sesualdum ad patrem Grimualdum trans Padum[56] direxit, obsecrans, ut quantocius veniret filioque suo ac Beneventanis, quos ipse nutrierat, potenter succurreret. Quod Grimuald rex audiens, statim cum exercitu filio laturus auxilium Beneventum pergere coepit. Quem plures ex Langobardis in itinere relinquentes, ad propria remearunt, dicentes, quia expoliasset palatium et iam non reversurus repeteret Beneventum.

(Book V, c.7a)

Turning the Tide

Interim imperatoris exercitus Beneventum diversis machinis vehementer expugnabat, econtra Romuald cum Langobardis fortiter resistebat. Qui quamvis cum tanta multitudine congredi manu ad manum propter paucitatem exercitus non auderet, frequenter tamen cum expeditis iuvenibus hostium castra inrumpens, magnas eisdem inferebat undique clades. Cumque Grimuald, eius pater, iamque properaret, eundem nutricium eius, de quo praemisimus, ad filium misit, qui ei suum adventum nuntiaret. Qui cum prope Beneventum venisset, a Grecis captus imperatori delatus est. Qui ab eo unde adveniret requirens, ille se a Grimualdo rege venire dixit eundemque regem citius adventare nuntiavit. Statimque imperator exterritus, consilium cum suis iniit, quatenus cum Romualdo pacisceretur, ut Neapolim possit reverti.

(Book V, c.7b)

---

[54] Agerentia—Acerenza

[55] For "iuvenulus," read "iuventulus."

[56] Padus—Po

Treacherous Greeks

Acceptaque obside Romualdi sororem, cui nomen Gisa fuit, cum eodem pacem fecit.[57] Eius vero nutricium Sesualdum ad muros duci praecepit, mortem eidem minatus, si aliquid Romualdo aut civibus de Grimualdi adventu nuntiaret, sed potius asseveraret, eundem venire minime posse. Quod ille ita se facturum ut ei praecipiebatur promisit; sed cum prope muros advenisset, velle se Romualdum videre dixit. Quo cum Romuald citius advenisset, sic ad eum locutus est: "Constans esto, domine Romuald, et habens fiduciam noli turbari, quia tuus genitor citius tibi auxilium praebiturus aderit. Nam scias, eum hac nocte iuxta Sangrum fluvium cum valido exercitu manere. Tantum obsecro, ut misericordiam exhibeas cum mea uxore et filiis, quia gens ista

Solidus of Constans II with Son

perfida me vivere non sinebit."[58] Cumque hoc dixisset, iussu imperatoris caput eius abscisum atque cum belli machina quam petrariam vocant in urbem proiectum est. Quod caput Romuald sibi deferri iussit idque lacrimans obsculatus est dignoque in loculo tumulari praecepit.[59]

(Book V, c.8)

---

[57] The rest of this chapter does not sound very peaceful. Paul seems to be following different sources here, and not merging them with his usual skill. Also, "sororem" should read "sorore."

[58] For "sinebit," read "sinet."

[59] Note the contrast here between shifty, degenerate Greeks and honourable Westerners. The Greeks force a man to lie, on pain of instant death, to his own nation's disadvantage. He refuses, sure that his family will be looked after. The Greeks kill him. Romuald is distraught. It is a contrast that contains much truth. In this war, the Easterners are at a local disadvantage. The overall balance of wealth and military power is heavily against the Westerners. Defeat is embarrassing for the Empire, but of no strategic significance. The contrast will be made again, however, four hundred years later, in the Second Crusade. By now, the balance of advantage has shifted. This time, the collapse of trust between the two halves of Christendom will not end well for the East.

The Empire Defeated

Metuens igitur imperator subitum Grimualdi regis adventum, dimissa Beneventi obsidione, Neapolim proficiscitur. Cuius tamen exercitum Mitola Capuanus comes iuxta fluenta Caloris fluminis in loco qui usque hodie Pugna dicitur vehementer adtrivit.

Postquam vero imperator Neapolim pervenit, unus ex eius optimatibus, cui nomen Saburrus erat, ab Augusto, ut fertur, viginti milia militum expetiit, seque cum Romualdo pugnaturum victoremque spopondit. Qui cum accepto exercitu ad locum cui Forinus nomen est advenisset ibique castra posuisset, Grimuald, qui iam Beneventum advenerat, haec audiens, contra eum proficisci voluit. Cui filius Romuald: "Non est opus;" inquit "sed tantum partem nobis de exercitu vestro tribuite. Ego Deo favente cum eo pugnabo; et cum vicero, maior utique gloria vestrae potentiae adscribetur." Factumque est; et accepta aliqua parte de patris exercitu, pariterque cum suis hominibus contra Saburrum proficiscitur. Qui priusquam bellum cum eo iniret, a quattuor partibus tubas insonare praecepit moxque super eos audenter inrupit. Cumque utraeque acies forti intentione pugnarent, tunc unus de regis exercitu nomine Amalongus, qui regium contum ferre erat solitus, quendam Greculum eodem contulo utrisque manibus fortiter percutiens, de sella super quam equitabat sustulit eumque in aera super caput suum levavit. Quod cernens Grecorum exercitus, mox inmenso pavore perterritus in fugam convertitur, ultimaque pernicie caesus, sibi fugiens mortem, Romualdo et Langobardis victoriam peperit. Ita Saburrus, qui se imperatori suo victoriae tropaeum de Langobardis promiserat patrare, ad eum cum paucis remeans, ignominiam deportavit; Romuald vero, patrata de inimicis victoria, Beneventum triumphans reversus est patrique gaudium et cunctis securitatem, sublato hostium timore, convexit.

(Book V, c.9-10)

An Imperial Sack of Rome

At vero Constans Augustus cum nihil se contra Langobardos gessisse conspiceret, omnes saevitiae suae minas contra suos, hoc est Romanos, retorsit. Nam egressus Neapoli, Romam perrexit.[60] Cui sexto ab urbe miliario Vitalianus papa cum sacerdotibus et Romano populo occurrit. Qui Augustus cum ad beati Petri limina pervenisset, optulit ibi pallium auro textile; et manens aput Romam diebus duodecim, omnia quae fuerant

---

[60] He entered Rome on the 5th July 663, the first Emperor to visit in two centuries.

antiquitus instituta ex aere in ornamentum civitatis deposuit, in tantum ut etiam basilicam beatae Mariae, quae aliquando Pantheum vocabatur et conditum fuerat in honore omnium deorum, et iam ibi per concessionem superiorum principum locus erat omnium martyrum, discooperiret tegulasque aereas exinde auferret easque simul cum aliis omnibus ornamentis Constantinopolim transmitteret.[61]

(Book V, c.11a)

The Pantheon

The Tyranny and Death of Constans

Deinde reversus imperator Neapolim, itinere terreno perrexit civitatem Regium. Ingressusque Siciliam per indictionem septimam, habitavit in Syracusa, et tales afflictiones inposuit populo seu habitatoribus vel possessoribus Calabriae, Siciliae, Africae atque Sardiniae, quales antea numquam auditae sunt, ita ut etiam uxores a maritis vel filii a parentibus separarentur.[62] Sed et alia multa et inaudita harum regionum populi sunt

---

[61] The Pantheon was saved from ruin because the Pope replaced the stolen roofing with tiles from the Temple of Jupiter. We shall see that the Arabs finally got the booty.

[62] Sold into slavery, it seems, to satisfy the demands of the tax gatherers.

perpessi, ita ut alicui spes vitae non remaneret. Nam et vasa sacrata vel cimelia sanctarum Dei ecclesiarum imperiali iussu et Grecorum avaricia sublata sunt. Mansit autem imperator in Sicilia ab indictione septima usque in duodecimam; sed tandem tantarum iniquitatum poenas luit, atque dum se in balneo lavaret, a suis extinctus est.[63]

(Book V, c.11b)

The Arabs Invade, Famine and Portents

Interfecto igitur aput Siracusas Constante imperatore, Mecetius in Sicilia regnum arripuit, sed absque orientalis exercitus voluntate.[64] Contra quem Italiae milites alii per Histriam, alii per partes Campaniae, alii vero a partibus Africae et Sardiniae venientes in Siracusas, eum vita privarunt. Multique ex iudicibus eius detruncati Constantinopolim perducti sunt; cum quibus pariter et falsi imperatoris caput est deportatum.

Haec audiens gens Sarracenorum, quae iam Alexandriam et Aegyptum pervaserat, subito cum multis navibus venientes, Siciliam invadunt, Siracusas ingrediuntur multamque stragem faciunt populorum, vix paucis evadentibus, qui per munitissima castra et iuga confugerant montium, auferentes quoque praedam nimiam et omne illud quod Constans Augustus a Roma abstulerat ornatum in aere et diversis speciebus; sicque Alexandriam reversi sunt.

Hoc tempore tantae pluviae tantaque tonitrua fuerunt, quanta ante nullus meminerat hominum, ita ut innumera hominum et animantium milia fulminibus essent perempta. Eo anno legumina, quae propter pluvias colligi nequiverunt, iterum renata et ad maturitatem usque perducta sunt.

Insequenti post tempore mense augusto a parte orientis stella cometis apparuit nimis fulgentibus radiis, quae post semet ipsam reversa disparuit. Nec mora, gravis pestilentia ab eadem parte orientis secuta, Romanum

---

[63] There are differing accounts of his death. The most entertaining is by Gibbon (c.48): "Odious to himself and to mankind, Constans perished by domestic, perhaps by episcopal, treason, in the capital of Sicily. A servant who waited in the bath, after pouring warm water on his head, struck him violently with the vase. He fell, stunned by the blow, and suffocated by the water; and his attendants, who wondered at the tedious delay, beheld with indifference the corpse of their lifeless emperor. The troops of Sicily invested with the purple an obscure youth, whose inimitable beauty eluded, and it might easily elude, the declining art of the painters and sculptors of the age."

[64] The 15th July 668.

populum devastavit. His diebus Domnus papa Romanae ecclesiae locum qui Paradisus dicitur ante basilicam beati apostoli Petri candidis et magnis marmoribus mirifice stravit.

(Book V, c.12,13,15,31)

The End of the Monothelite Heresy

Dum haec in Italia geruntur, heresis aput Constantinopolim orta est, quae unam in domino nostro Iesu Christo voluntatem et operationem adseverabat. Hanc autem heresem excitarunt Georgius patriarcha Constantinopolitanus, Macharius, Pyrrus, Paulus et Petrus. Quam ob causam Constantinus Augustus centum quinquaginta episcopos congregari fecit; inter quos etiam fuerunt legati sanctae Romanae ecclesiae missi ab Agathone papa, Iohannes diaconus et Iohannes Portuensis episcopus; qui omnes eandem heresem damnaverunt. [65] Ea hora tantae haranearum telae in medio populi ceciderunt, ut omnes mirarentur; ac per hoc significatum est, quod sordes hereticae pravitatis depulsae sunt. Et Georgius quidem patriarcha correptus est, ceteri vero in sua defensione perseverantes anathematis sunt ultione perculsi. Eo

---

[65] The Sixth Ecumenical Council took place in 680. Following its establishment by Constantine, the Early Church fell into centuries of dispute over the Nature of Christ. First, there was the Arian controversy, in which the relationship between God and Christ was disputed. After this came the Monophysite controversy, in which the relationship of Christ and man was disputed. These controversies were serious in their effects, as the various sides often corresponded to the racial and linguistic divisions within the Empire. For example, the Greeks and Latins stood by the Council of Chalcedon (451), according to which, Christ was "perfect both in deity and in humanness; this self-same one is also actually God and actually man." The Syrian and Egyptian semites tended to the Monophysite view of Christ as at least greatly more divine than human.

The Monothelite doctrine was an Imperial attempt to settle the Monophysite controversy. Four successive patriarchs of Constantinople had approved the new doctrine. However, the Western Church was united against it. Also, by the end of the seventh century, the Arab conquests had made it redundant: there were hardly any semites who needed to be reconciled.

Therefore, the Emperor asked the Pope to send delegates to an Ecumenical Council. Macarius, Patriarch of Antioch, tried to prove that the dogma of "one theandric energy" was in harmony with the decisions of the Fourth and Fifth Councils. But the genuineness of some of his quotations was denied and the relevancy of others disputed. Gregory, Patriarch of Constantinople, formally sided with the Papal delegates, who insisted that Christ had two wills, human and divine. The decrees of Pope Agatho and the Western Synod were ratified, Macarius was deposed and the projectors of what was now the Monothelete heresy were condemned, including Honorius, a former Pope.

These matters are extensively covered in: Richard Blake, *Ghosts of Athens*, Hodder & Stoughton, London, 2011.

tempore Damianus Ticinensis ecclesiae episcopus sub nomine Mansueti Mediolanensis archiepiscopi hac de causa satis utilem rectaeque fidei epistolam conposuit, quae in praefato sinodo non mediocre suffragium tulit. Recta autem et vera fides haec est, ut in domino nostro Iesu Christo sicut duae sunt naturae, hoc est Dei et hominis, sic etiam duae credantur esse voluntates sive operationes. Vis audire de eo quod deitatis est? Ego, inquit, et pater unum sumus. Vis audire quod humanitatis? Pater maior me est. Cerne secundum humanitatem eum in navi dormientem; cerne eius divinitatem cum evangelista ait: Tunc surgens imperavit ventis et mari, et facta est tranquillitas magna. Haec est sexta sinodus universalis Constantinopoli celebrata et Greco sermone conscripta, temporibus papae Agathonis, exsequente ac residente Constantino principe intra septa palatii sui.

(Book VI, c.4)

More Portents, More Plague

His temporibus per indictionem octavam luna eclypsin passa est.[66] Solis quoque eclypsis eodem pene tempore, hora diei quasi decima, quinto nonas maias effecta est. Moxque subsecuta gravissima pestis est tribus mensibus, hoc est iulio, augusto et septembrio; tantaque fuit multitudo morientium, ut etiam parentes cum filiis atque fratres cum sororibus, bini per feretra positi, aput urbem Romam ad sepulchra ducerentur. Pari etiam modo haec pestilentia Ticinum quoque depopulata est, ita ut, cunctis civibus per iuga montium seu per diversa loca fugientibus, in foro et per plateas civitatis herbae et frutecta nascerentur. Tuncque visibiliter multis apparuit, quia bonus et malus angelus noctu per civitatem pergerent, et ex iussu boni angeli malus angelus, qui videbatur venabulum manu ferre, quotiens de venabulo ostium cuiuscumque domus percussisset, tot de eadem domo die sequenti homines interirent. Tunc cuidam per revelationem dictum est, quod pestis ipsa prius non quiesceret, quam in basilica beati Petri quae ad Vincula dicitur sancti Sebastiani martyris altarium poneretur. Factumque est, et delatis ab urbe Roma beati Sebastiani martyris reliquiis, mox ut in iam dicta basilica altarium constitutum est, pestis ipsa quievit.

(Book VI, c.5)

---

[66] The 2nd May 681.

The Siege of Ravenna and the Iconoclast Controversy

Eoque tempore rex Liutprandus Ravennam obsedit, Classem invasit atque destruxit. Tunc Paulus patricius ex Ravenna misit qui pontificem interemerent; sed Langobardis pro defensione pontificis repugnantibus, Spoletinis in Salario ponte et ex aliis partibus Langobardis Tuscis resistentibus, consilium Ravennantium dissipatum est. Hac tempestate Leo imperator aput Constantinopolim sanctorum imagines depositas incendit Romanoque pontifici similia facere, si imperialem gratiam habere vellet, mandavit. Sed pontifex hoc facere contempsit. Omnis quoque Ravennae exercitus vel Venetiarum[67] talibus iussis uno animo restiterunt, et nisi eos pontifex prohibuisset, imperatorem super se constituere sunt adgressi.[68] Rex quoque Liutprand castra Emiliae, Feronianum et Montembellium, Buxeta et Persiceta, Bononiam et Pentapolim Auximumque invasit. Pari quoque modo tunc et Sutrium pervasit. Sed post aliquot dies iterum Romanis redditum est. Per idem tempus Leo Augustus ad peiora progressus est, ita ut conpelleret omnes Constantinopolim habitantes tam vi quam blandimentis, ut deponerent ubicumque haberentur imagines tam Salvatoris quamque eius sanctae genetricis vel omnium sanctorum, easque in medium civitatis incendio concremari fecit. Et quia plerique ex populo tale scelus fieri praepediebant, aliquanti ex eis capite truncati, alii parte corporis multati sunt. Cuius errori Germanus patriarcha non consentiens, a propria sede depulsus est, et eius in loco Anastasius presbiter ordinatus est.

(Book VI, c.49)

---

[67] This word is the plural, "the Venices." There were then two Venices—land Venice, mostly under the Lombards, and sea Venice, under the Empire.

[68] This controversy dates from the time of Gregory I. The weakness of the Empire gave the Papacy an increasingly political character. Gregory extended his influence, even trying to make a separate peace with the Lombards, an act resented by the Emperor Maurice (582-602). The people of Italy began to look to a new Empire of the West. The usurpation of the Exarch Eleutherius (618) and the subsequent rebellion of Olympius, supported by Pope Martin I, show this separatist tendency. Ecclesiastical differences such as the assumption of the title of Universal Bishop by the Patriarch of Constantinople, the Monothelete controversy, the imprisonment of Pope Martin, and so forth, caused further irritation in the West.

Constantine Pogonatus (Emperor: 668-85) had adopted a policy of friendship with the Papacy, and made peace with the Lombards, fixing their mutual boundaries in Italy. However, the Lombards then abandoned Arianism for Catholicism, and the Popes began to play the Lombards and the Empire against each other. Then came the Iconoclast controversy after 725. This sent diplomatic and religious and military affairs into more turmoil than this commentary has room to explore. But we are now approaching the moment when not a Lombard King, but the Frankish King, Charles the Great, is persuaded to Rome, and a new age in the history of Europe is definitely opened—on the 25th December 800.

The Arabs Invade France, but are Defeated

Per idem tempus Sarracenorum exercitus rursum in Galliam introiens, multam devastationem fecit. Contra quos Carolus non longe a Narbone bellum committens, eos sicut et prius maxima caede prostravit. Iterato Sarraceni Gallorum fines ingressi, usque ad Provinciam venerunt, et capta Arelate, omnia circumquaque demoliti sunt. Tunc Carolus legatos cum muneribus ad Liutprandum regem mittens, ab eo contra Sarracenos auxilium poposcit; qui nihil moratus cum omni Langobardorum exercitu in eius adiutorium properavit. Quo conperto gens Sarracenorum mox ab illis regionibus aufugit;[69] Liutprandus vero cum omni suo exercitu ad Italiam rediit. Insequenti quoque tempore Romani, elatione solita turgidi, congregati universaliter, habentes in capite Agathonem Perusinorum ducem, venerunt ut Bononiam conprehenderent, ubi tunc Walcari, Peredeo et Rotcari morabantur in castris. Qui super Romanos inruentes, multam de eis stragem fecerunt reliquosque fugam petere conpulerunt. Multa idem regnator contra Romanos bella gessit, in quibus semper victor extitit, praeter quod semel in Arimino eo absente eius exercitus caesus est, et alia vice, cum aput vicum Pilleum, rege in Pentapoli demorante, magna multitudo horum qui regi munuscula vel exenia vel singularum ecclesiarum benedictiones deferebant, a Romanis inruentibus caesa vel capta est. Rursus cum Ravennam Hildeprandus, regis nepos, et Peredeo Vicentinus dux optinerent, inruentibus subito Veneticis, Hildeprandus ab eis captus est, Peredo viriliter pugnans occubuit.

(Book VI, c.54)

---

[69] The Battle of Narbonne took place in 737, between the forces of Charles Martel (ruled: 718-41) and the Arabs, who had taken Spain after 711. Despite their defeat at Tours in 732, the Arabs remained in control of Narbonne and Septimania for another twenty seven years, though they could not expand further. The treaties reached earlier with the local population stood firm and were further consolidated in 734 when the governor of Narbonne, Yusuf ibn 'Abd al-Rahman al-Fihri, concluded agreements with several towns on common defence arrangements against the encroachments of Charles Martel, who had systematically brought the south to heel as he extended his domains. The army attempting to relieve Narbonne met Charles in battle at the Battle of the River Berre and was destroyed. However, Charles failed to take Narbonne by siege in 737, when the city was jointly defended by the Arabs and its Christian Visigothic citizens.

POSTSCRIPT

Many thanks for buying this book. Many thanks for reading it. Sales of my books are useful to my finances, and they help assure me that I have not been typing away without hope of influence and fame. If you liked it, please consider leaving a review on your local Amazon. Reviews are very important for further sales. Even if you disagree with what I have said, please go ahead and review the book.

You may also wish to look up some of my other books on Amazon. There are many of these. Under my own name, Sean Gabb, I write both non-fiction and fiction. Under the pen-name, Richard Blake, I am writing a long series of historical novels set in the early Byzantine Empire. There are now twelve of these, and they have been commercially translated into half a dozen languages.

Though not overtly political, they do manage to reflect my general view of life, and may be of interest. I might add that, in hard copy, they make interesting presents for those hard-to-please loved ones!

Otherwise, please feel free to connect with me on Facebook and on various other social media platforms. Or feel free to contact me directly—*sean@seangabb.co.uk* or via my websites:

https://www.seangabb.co.uk/
http://www.richardblake.me.uk/
http://www.classicstuition.co.uk/

Best regards,

Sean Gabb
Deal

VOCABULARY

a, ab *prep abl* by (agent), from (departure, cause, remote origin, time); after (reference);

a *prep acc* ante, *abb*. a.; [in calendar expression a. d. = ante diem => before the day];

abavia, abaviae *n* (1st) *f* ancestress; great-great grandmother;

abbas, abbatis *n* (3rd) *m* abbot; head of an ecclesiastical community; father; any respected monk (early);

abbatia, abbatiae *n* (1st) *f* abbey, monastery;

abbatissa, abbatissae *n* (1st) *f* abbess;

abdo, abdere, abdidi, abditus *v* (3rd) *trans* remove, put away, set aside; depart, go away; hide, keep secret, conceal;

abduco, abducere, abduxi, abductus *v* (3rd) *trans* lead away, carry off; detach, attract away, entice, seduce, charm; withdraw;

abeo, abire, abivi(ii), abitus *v intrans* depart, go away; go off, go forth; pass away, die, disappear; be changed;

abfero, abferre, -, - *v trans* bear, take away, remove, obtain, carry off, away, steal; (error for aufero);

abfluo, abfluere, abfluxi, - *v* (3rd) *intrans* flow, stream, issue (from); flow away; be abundant, abound (in w, *abl*);

abfugio, abfugere, abfugi, - *v* (3rd) flee (from), shun; run, fly away, escape; disappear, vanish (things);

abhibeo, abhibere, -, - *v* (2nd) *trans* hold at a distance;

abhinc *adv* since, ago, in past; from this time, henceforth; from this place, hence;

abicio, abicere, abieci, abiectus *v* (3rd) *trans* throw, cast away, down, aside; abandon; slight; humble; debase; sell too cheaply;

abico, abicere, -, - *v* (3rd) *trans* humble; cast aside, away, off, reject;

ablatio, ablationis *n* (3rd) *f* removal, taking away;

ablegatio, ablegationis *n* (3rd) *f* dispatch, sending away, off; dispatch on a duty;

ablego, ablegare, ablegavi, ablegatus *v* (1st) *trans* send away, off (on a mission); banish, get

abscido, abscidere, abscidi, abscisus *v* (3rd) *trans* hew, cut off, away, out; fell, cut down; remove, separate, cut off, destroy, divide; take away violently; expel, banish; destroy (hope); amputate; prune; cut short;

abscindo, abscindere, abscidi, abscissus *v* (3rd) *trans* tear (away, off) (clothing); cut off, away, short; part, break, divide, separate;

abscondeo, abscondere, abscondui, absconditus *v* (2nd) hide, conceal, secrete, "shelter"; leave behind; bury, engulf, swallow up; keep;

abscondite *adv* abstrusely; profoundly; secretly;

absconditum, absconditi *n* (2nd) *n* hidden, secret, concealed place, thing; secret;

absconditus, abscondita, absconditum *adi* hidden, secret, concealed; covert, disguised; abstruse, recondite;

abscondo, abscondere, abscondi, absconditus *v* (3rd) hide, conceal, secrete, "shelter"; leave behind; bury, engulf, swallow up; keep;

absimilis, absimilis, absimile *adi* unlike, dissimilar;

absque *prep abl* without, apart from, away from; but for; except for; were it not for; (early);

abstraho, abstrahere, abstraxi, abstractus *v* (3rd) *trans* drag away from, remove forcibly, abort; carry off to execution; split;

absum, abesse, abfui, abfuturus *v* be away, absent, distant, missing; be free, removed from; be lacking; be distinct;

abundanter, abundantius, abundantissime *adv* abundantly; profusely, copiously; on a lavish scale;

abundantia, abundantiae *n* **(1st)** *f* abundance, plenty; riches; fullness; overflow, excess; discharge (of blood);

ac *coni* and, and also, and besides;

accedo, accedere, accessi, accessus *v* **(3rd)** come near, approach; agree with; be added to (w, *ad* or *in* + *acc*); constitute;

accipio, accipere, accepi, acceptus *v* **(3rd)** *trans* take, grasp, receive, accept, undertake; admit, let in, hear, learn; obey;

acies, aciei *n* **(5th)** *f* sharpness, sharp edge, point; battle line, array; sight, glance; pupil of eye;

actum *adv* sharply, pointedly; acutely;

actum, acti *n* **(2nd)** *n* act, deed, transaction; acts (pl.), exploits; chronicles, (official) record;

actus, actus *n* **(4th)** *m* act, performance (of play), delivery; action, deed; series, sequence; progress; right of way, road for cattle; path, cart-track; land measure (120 ft.);

acumen, acuminis *n* **(3rd)** *n* sharpened point, spur; sting; peak, promontory; sharpness, cunning, acumen; fraud;

ad *adv* about (with numerals);

ad *prep acc* to, up to, towards; near, at; until, on, by; almost; according to; about w, NUM;

addico, addicere, addixi, addictus *v* **(3rd)** *trans* be propitious; adjudge, sentence, doom; confiscate; award, assign; enslave;

addictus, addicta -um, addictior -or -us, addictissimus -a -um *adi* devoted, addicted (to); (debt) slave (of); bound (to do something); bent upon;

adduco, adducere, adduxi, adductus *v* **(3rd)** *trans* lead up, to, away; bring up, to; persuade, induce; lead, bring; contract, tighten;

adeo *adv* to such a degree, pass, point; precisely, exactly; thus far; indeed, truly, even;

adeo, adire, adivi(ii), aditus *v* approach; attack; visit, address; undertake; take possession (inheritance);

adfigo, adfigere, adfixi, adfixus *v* **(3rd)** *trans* fasten, fix, pin, attach to (w, *dat*), annex; impress upon; pierce; chain, confine;

adfligo, adfligere, adflixi, adflictus *v* **(3rd)** *trans* overthrow, throw down; afflict, damage, crush, break, ruin; humble, weaken, vex;

adgravo, adgravare, adgravavi, adgravatus *v* **(1st)** *trans* aggravate, exaggerate; weigh down, oppress; make heavier; embarrass further;

adgredio, adgredere, aggressi, aggressus *v* **(3rd)** *intrans* approach, advance; attack, assail; undertake, seize (opportunity), attempt;

adhaereo, adhaerere, adhaesi, adhaesus *v* **(2nd)** *intrans* adhere, stick, cling, cleave to; hang on; be attached, concerned, involved;

adhibeo, adhibere, adhibui, adhibitus *v* **(2nd)** *trans* summon, invite, bring in; consult; put, add; use, employ, apply; hold out to;

adhuc *adv* thus far, till now, to this point; hitherto; yet, as yet; still; besides;

adicio, adicere, adieci, adiectus *v* **(3rd)** *trans* add, increase, raise; add to (*dat*, *ad+acc*); suggest; hurl (weapon); throw to, at;

adiutor, adiutari, adiutatus sum *v* **(1st)** *dep* help (w, burden, activity); help realize a program, purpose;

adiutor, adiutoris *n* **(3rd)** *m* assistant, deputy; accomplice; supporter; secretary; assistant schoolmaster;

adiutorium, adiutori(i) *n* **(2nd)** *n* help, assistance, support; argumentation;

adloquor, adloqui, adlocutus sum *v* **(3rd)** *dep* speak to (friendly); address, harangue, make a speech (to); call on; console;

admoneo, admonere, admonui, admonitus *v* **(2nd)** *trans* admonish, remind, prompt; suggest, advise, raise; persuade, urge; warn, caution;

adnitor, adniti, adnisus sum *v* **(3rd)** *dep* lean, rest upon, support oneself, (w, genibus) kneel; strive, work, exert, try;

adnitor, adniti, adnixus sum *v* **(3rd)** *dep* lean, rest upon, support oneself, (w, genibus) kneel; strive, work, exert, try;

adolor, adolari, adolatus sum *v* **(1st)** *dep* fawn upon (as dog); flatter (in servile manner), court; make obeisance (to);

adoro, adorare, adoravi, adoratus *v* **(1st)** *trans* honour, adore, worship, pay homage, reverence; beg, plead with, appeal to;

adprehendo, adprehendere, adprehendi, adprehensus *v* **(3rd)** *trans* seize (upon), grasp, cling to, lay hold of; apprehend; embrace; overtake;

adscio, adscire, -, - v (4th) *trans* take to, up; associate, admit; adopt as one's own; take upon (General's) staff;

adscribo, adscribere, adscripsi, adscriptus v (3rd) *trans* add, state in writing, insert; appoint; enroll, enfranchise; reckon, number;

adsensio, adsensionis n (3rd) *f* assent, agreement, belief; approval, approbation, applause;

adsequor, adsequi, adsecutus sum v (3rd) *dep* follow on, pursue, go after; overtake; gain, achieve; equal, rival; understand;

adsevero, adseverare, adseveravi, adseveratus v (1st) *trans* act earnestly; assert strongly, emphatically, declare; profess; be serious;

adsto, adstare, adsteti, adstatus v (1st) *intrans* stand at, on, by, near; assist; stand up, upright, waiting, still, on one's feet;

adsum, adesse, adfui, adfuturus v be near, be present, be in attendance, arrive, appear; aid (w, dat);

adtribuo, adtribuere, adtribui, adtributus v (3rd) *trans* assign, allot, attribute, impute to; grant, pay; appoint, put under jurisdiction;

adulescens, adulescentis n (3rd) *c* young man, youth; youthful person; young woman, girl;

adulter, adulteri n (2nd) *m* adulterer; illicit lover, paramour; offspring of unlawful love, bastard (eccl.);

advenio, advenire, adveni, adventus v (4th) *intrans* come to, arrive; arrive at, reach, be brought; develop, set in, arise;

advento, adventare, adventavi, adventatus v (1st) *intrans* approach, come to, draw near; arrive, "turn up"; come in (tide); approximate;

adventus, adventus n (4th) *m* arrival, approach; visit, appearance, advent; ripening; invasion, incursion;

adversum *adv* opposite, against, in opposite direction; in opposition; (w, ire go to meet);

adversum *prep* *acc* facing, opposite, against, towards; contrary to; face to face, in presence of;

adversum, adversi n (2nd) *n* direction, point opposite, facing; uphill slope, direction; obstacle, trouble;

aedificialis, aedificialis, aedificiale *adi*

pertaining to a building;

aemulus, aemuli n (2nd) *m* rival, competitor, love rival; diligent imitator, follower; equal, peer;

aequum, aequi n (2nd) *n* level ground; equal footing, terms; what is right, fair, equitable, equity;

aer, aeris n c air (one of 4 elements); atmosphere, sky; cloud, mist, weather; breeze; odor;

aera, aerae n (1st) *f* darnel (grass, weed, grows among wheat, subject to ergot, thereby dangerous); arameter from which a calculation is made; item of account; era, epoch;

aerugo, aeruginis n (3rd) *f* rust of copper, verdigris; canker of the mind, envy, ill-will, avarice;

aes, aeris n (3rd) *n* money, pay, fee, fare; copper, bronze, brass, base metal; (w, alienum) debt; gong;

aestas, aestatis n (3rd) *f* summer; summer heat, weather; a year;

aestivalis, aestivalis, aestivale *adi* of summer, designed for summer use;

aestivo, aestivare, aestivavi, aestivatus v (1st) *intrans* spend, pass the summer;

aestuo, aestuare, aestuavi, aestuatus v (1st) *intrans* boil, seethe, foam; billow roll in waves; be agitated, hot; burn; waver;

aestus, aestus n (4th) *m* agitation, passion, seething; raging, boiling; heat, fire; sea tide, spray, swell;

affero, afferre, attuli, allatus v *trans* bring to (word, food), carry, convey; report, allege, announce; produce, cause;

afflictio, afflictionis n (3rd) *f* pain, suffering, torment;

affligo, affligere, afflixi, afflictus v (3rd) *trans* overthrow, throw down; afflict, damage, crush, break, ruin; humble, weaken, vex;

ager, agri n (2nd) *m* field, ground; farm, land, estate, park; territory, country; terrain; soil;

agmen, agminis n (3rd) *n* stream; herd, flock, troop, crowd; marching army, column, line; procession;

agnomen, agnominis n (3rd) *n* nickname, an additional name denoting an achievement, characteristic;

ago, agere, egi, actus v (3rd) drive, urge,

conduct, act; spend (time w, cum); thank (w, gratias); deliver (speech);

agrestis, agrestis *n* **(3rd)** *m* countryman, peasant; rube, rustic, bumpkin;

aio, -, - *v* say (defective), assert; say yes, so, affirm, assent; prescribe, lay down (law);

ait, -, - *v impers* he says (ait), it is said; they say (aiunt);

aleo, aleonis *n* **(3rd)** *m* gambler;

alia *adv* by another, different way, route;

alias *adv* at, in another time, place; previously, subsequently; elsewhere; otherwise;

alimonia, alimoniae *n* **(1st)** *f* food, nourishment; feeding, nurture, upbringing; cost of maintenance;

aliqua *adv* somehow, in some way or another, by some means or other; to some extent;

aliquando *adv* sometime (or other), at any time, ever; finally; before too late; at length;

aliquantulum *adv* to a little, small amount, bit, extent; slightly, somewhat;

aliquantus, aliquanta, aliquantum *adi* certain quantity, amount, number, size of; quite a quantity of; moderate;

aliquis, aliquis, aliquid *pron* anyone, anybody, anything; someone, something; one or another;

aliquod, undeclined *adi* some, several; a few; not many; a number (of); more than one;

aliquod, undeclined *n* N some, several, a few people; more than one; a number;

aliquot, undeclined *adi* some, several; a few; not many; a number (of); more than one;

aliquot, undeclined *n* N some, several, a few people; more than one; a number;

aliter *adv* otherwise, differently; in any other way [aliter ac => otherwise than];

altarium, altarii *n* **(2nd)** *n* altar; high altar;

alter *coni* the_one ... the_other (alter ... alter); otherwise;

alter, altera, alterum *adi* one (of two); second, another; former, latter; [unus et ~=> one or two, other]; second, further, next, other, latter, some person, thing (*pronominal adj*); either;

alternatim *adv* by turns, alternately;

altus, alta -um, altior -or -us, altissimus -a -um *adi* high; deep, profound; shrill; lofty,

noble; deep rooted; far-fetched; grown great;

alveus, alvei *n* **(2nd)** *m* cavity, hollow; tub; trough, bowl, tray; gameboard; beehive; canoe; hold (ship), ship, boat; channel, bed (river), trench;

amens, amentis (gen.), amentior -or -us, amentissimus -a -um *adi* insane, demented, out of one's mind; very excited, frantic, distracted; foolish;

amentia, amentiae *n* **(1st)** *f* madness; extreme folly, infatuation, stupidity; frenzy, violent excitement;

amicus, amica -um, amicior -or -us, amicissimus -a -um *adi* friendly, dear, fond of; supporting (political), loyal, devoted; loving;

amicus, amici *n* **(2nd)** *m* friend, ally, disciple; loved one; patron; counselor, courtier (to a prince);

ammirator, ammiratoris *n* **(3rd)** *m* admirer; one who venerates;

ammitto, ammittere, ammisi, ammissus *v* **(3rd)** *trans* urge on, put to a gallop; let in, admit, receive; grant, permit, let go;

amor, amoris *n* **(3rd)** *m* love; affection; the beloved; Cupid; affair; sexual, illicit, homosexual passion;

amotio, amotionis *n* **(3rd)** *f* removal; deprivation; process of removing;

amplitudo, amplitudinis *n* **(3rd)** *f* greatness; extent, breadth, width, bulk; importance; fullness (of expression);

amplius, undeclined *adi* greater (w, indef. subject, eg., number than), further, more, longer;

anathema, anathematis *n* **(3rd)** *n* offering; sacrificial victim; curse; cursed thing; excommunication, anathema;

angario, angariare, angariavi, angariatus *v* **(1st)** *trans* press, requisition, commandeer; exact villeinage; compel, constrain (eccl.);

angelus, angeli *n* **(2nd)** *m* angel; messenger;

angustus, angusta -um, angustior -or -us, angustissimus -a -um *adi* narrow, steep, close, confined; scanty, poor; low, mean; narrowminded, petty;

anima, animae *n* **(1st)** *f* soul, spirit, vital principle; life; breathing; wind, breeze; air (element);

animadverto,   animadvertere, animadverti, animadversus *v* **(3rd)** pay attention to, attend to; notice, observe; judge, estimate; punish (in+*acc*);

animal, animalis *n* **(3rd)** *n* animal, living thing, offspring; creature, beast, brute; insect;

animans, (gen.), animantis *adi* living, having life;

animans, animantis *n* **(3rd)** *c* animate, living being, organism (not man), creature; animal, plant;

animositas, animositatis *n* **(3rd)** *f* boldness, courage, spirit; vehemence, impetuosity, ardor; wrath (eccl.);

animus, animi *n* **(2nd)** *m* mind; intellect; soul; feelings; heart; spirit, courage, character, pride; air;

annualis, annualis, annuale *adi* one year old;

annus, anni *n* **(2nd)** *m* year (astronomical, civil); age, time of life; year's produce; circuit, course;

ante *adv* before, previously, first, before this, earlier; in front, advance of; forwards;

ante *prep acc* in front, presence of, in view; before (space, time, degree); over against, facing;

antea *adv* before, before this; formerly, previously, in the past;

anterior, anterior, anterius *adi* earlier, previous, former; that is before, foremost;

anticipatio, anticipationis *n* **(3rd)** *f* preconception, previous notion; anticipation; idea before receiving instruction;

antiquitas, antiquitatis *n* **(3rd)** *f* antiquity, the good old days; the ancients; virtues of olden times; being old;

antiquitus, antiquita -um, antiquitior -or -us, antiquitissimus -a -um *adi* old, ancient, aged; time-honoured; simple, classic; venerable; archaic, outdated;

antrum, antri *n* **(2nd)** *n* cave; cavern; hollow place with overarching foliage; cavity, hollow; tomb;

aperio, aperire, aperui, apertus *v* **(4th)** *trans* uncover, open, disclose; explain, recount; reveal; found; excavate; spread out;

apostolicus, apostolica, apostolicum *adi* apostolic; of, concerning, belonging to an Apostle; title applied to Pope;

apostolus, apostoli *n* **(2nd)** *m* apostle; missionary (one sent);

appareo, apparere, apparui, apparitus *v* **(2nd)** *intrans* appear; be evident, visible, noticed, found; show up, occur; serve (w, *dat*);

appello, appellere, appuli, appulsus *v* **(3rd)** drive to, move up, bring along, force towards; put ashore at, land (ship);

applico, applicare, applicui, applicitus *v* **(1st)** *trans* connect, place near, bring into contact; land (ship); adapt; apply, devote to;

aptus, apta -um, aptior -or -us, aptissimus -a -um *adi* suitable, adapted; ready; apt, proper; tied, attached to; dependent on (w, ex);

apud *prep acc* at, by, near, among; at the house of; before, in the presence, writings, view of;

aput *prep acc* at, by, near, among; at the house of; before, in presence, writings, view, eyes of;

aqua, aquae *n* **(1st)** *f* water; sea, lake; river, stream; rain, rainfall (pl.), rainwater; spa; urine;

aquilo, aquilonis *n* **(3rd)** *m* north wind; NNE, NE wind (for Rome); north; Boreas (personified);

arbitror, arbitrari, arbitratus sum *v* **(1st)** *dep* observe, witness; testify; decide, judge, sentence; believe, think, imagine;

archiepiscopus, archiepiscopi *n* **(2nd)** *m* archbishop;

Arctos, Arcti *n* *f* Big, Little Dipper, Bear, region of celestial pole; North lands, people, direction;

arcus, arcus *n* **(4th)** *m* bow, arc, coil, arch; rainbow; anything arched or curved;

argentatus, argentata, argentatum *adi* silvered, adorned with silver; concerned with money;

argumentatio, argumentationis *n* **(3rd)** *f* arguing, presentation of arguments; line of argument, particular proof;

armatus, armata -um, armatior -or -us, armatissimus -a -um *adi* armed, equipped; defensively armed, armour clad; fortified; of the use of arms;

armiger, armigeri *n* **(2nd)** *m* armour bearer; squire; [Iovis armiger => Jupiter's armour-bearer = the eagle];

arripio, arripere, arripui, arreptus *v* **(3rd)** *trans* take hold of; seize (hand, tooth, claw), snatch; arrest; assail; pick up, absorb;

ars, artis *n* **(3rd)** *f* skill, craft, art; trick, wile; science, knowledge; method, way; character (pl.);

arva, arvae *n* **(1st)** *f* arable land, plowed field; soil, region; countryside; dry land; lowlands, plain;

arvus, arva, arvum *adi* arable (land); cultivated, plowed;

arx, arcis *n* **(3rd)** *f* citadel, stronghold, city; height, hilltop; Capitoline hill; defense, refuge;

ascendo, ascendere, ascendi, ascensus *v* **(3rd)** climb; go, climb up; mount, scale; mount up, embark; rise, ascend, move upward;

aspicio, aspicere, aspexi, aspectus *v* **(3rd)** *trans* look, gaze on, at, see, observe, behold, regard; face; consider, contemplate;

assequor, assequi, assecutus sum *v* **(3rd)** *dep* follow on, pursue, go after; overtake; gain, achieve; equal, rival; understand;

assevero, asseverare, asseveravi, asseveratus *v* **(1st)** *trans* act earnestly; assert strongly, emphatically, declare; profess; be serious;

at *coni* but, but on the other hand; on the contrary; while, whereas; but yet; at least;

atque *coni* and, as well, soon as; together with; and moreover, even; and too, also, now; yet;

attonitus, attonita, attonitum *adi* astonished, fascinated; lightning, thunder-struck, stupefied, dazed; inspired;

attritus, attrita -um, attritior -or -us, attritissimus -a -um *adi* worn, worn down by use; smoothed; hardened, brazen; thin (style), attenuated; rubbed (off, away), wasted; bruised; shameless, impudent, brazen;

auctor, auctoris *n* **(3rd)** *c* seller, vendor; originator; historian; authority; proposer, supporter; founder;

audacia, audaciae *n* **(1st)** *f* boldness, daring, courage, confidence; recklessness, effrontery, audacity;

audacter, audacius, audacissime *adv* boldly, audaciously, confidently, proudly, fearlessly; impudently, rashly;

audenter, audentius, audentissime *adv* boldly, fearlessly; audaciously, presumptuously, rashly;

audio, audire, audivi, auditus *v* **(4th)** hear, listen, accept, agree with; obey; harken, pay attention; be able to hear;

audo, audere, - *v* *semidep* intend, be prepared; dare, have courage (to go, do), act boldly, venture, risk;

aufero, auferre, abstuli, ablatus *v* *trans* bear, carry, take, fetch, sweep, snatch away, off, remove, withdraw; steal, obtain;

aufugio, aufugere, aufugi, - *v* **(3rd)** flee, flee from, shun; run, fly away, escape; disappear (things), vanish;

augeo, augere, auxi, auctus *v* **(2nd)** *trans* increase, enlarge, augment; spread; honour, promote, raise; exalt; make a lot of;

aurum, auri *n* **(2nd)** *n* gold (metal, colour), gold money, riches;

ausus, ausus *n* **(4th)** *m* daring, initiative; ventures (pl.);

aut *coni* or, or rather, else; either...or (aut...aut) (emphasizing one);

autem *coni* but (postpositive), on the other hand, contrary; while, however; moreover, also;

auxilium, auxili(i) *n* **(2nd)** *n* help, assistance; remedy, antidote; supporting resource, force; auxiliaries (pl.);

avaritia, avaricia, avaritiae *n* **(1st)** *f* greed, avarice; rapacity; miserliness, stinginess, meanness;

averto, avertere, averti, aversus *v* **(3rd)** turn away from, aside, divert, rout; disturb; withdraw; steal, misappropriate;

avus, avi *n* **(2nd)** *m* grandfather; forefather, ancestor;

axis, axis *n* **(3rd)** *m* axle, axis, pole; chariot; the sky, heaven; north pole; region, clime;

balneum, balnei *n* **(2nd)** *n* bath; bathtub; act of bathing; bathroom, (public) bath place, rooms (esp. pl.);

baptista, baptistae *n* **(1st)** *m* baptizer; baptist;

barba, barbae *n* **(1st)** *f* beard, whiskers; large unkempt beard (pl.); [Jovis ~ => shrub Anthyllis barba];

barbarus, barbara -um, barbarior -or -us, barbarissimus -a -um *adi* foreign, of, used by, typical of foreigners; cruel, savage; uncivilized, uncouth;

barbarus, barbari *n* **(2nd)** *m* barbarian, uncivilized person; foreigner (not Greek, Roman);

basilica, basilicae *n* **(1st)** *f* basilica; oblong

hall with colonnade as law court, exchange; church (mediaeval);

beatus, beata -um, beatior -or -us, beatissimus -a -um *adi* happy, fortunate, bringing happiness; rich, wealthy, copious, sumptuous;

bellator, bellatoris *n* **(3rd)** *m* warrior, fighter; soldier;

bellicosus, bellicosa -um, bellicosior -or -us, bellicosissimus -a -um *adi* warlike, fierce; fond of war;

bellua, belluae *n* **(1st)** *f* beast, wild animal (incl. sea creature); monster, brute (great size, ferocity);

bellum, belli *n* **(2nd)** *n* war, warfare; battle, combat, fight; (at, in) (the) war(s); military force, arms;

bellus, bella -um, bellior -or -us, bellissimus -a -um *adi* pretty, handsome, charming, pleasant, agreeable, polite; nice, fine, excellent;

belua, beluae *n* **(1st)** *f* beast, wild animal (incl. sea creature); monster, brute (great size, ferocity);

bene, melius, optime *adv* well, very, quite, rightly, agreeably, cheaply, in good style; better; best;

benedictio, benedictionis *n* **(3rd)** *f* blessing; benediction; extolling, praising; consecrated, sacred object;

beneficium, benefici(i) *n* **(2nd)** *n* kindness, favour, benefit, service, help; privilege, right;

bestia, bestiae *n* **(1st)** *f* beast, animal, creature; wild beast, animal, beast of prey in arena;

bibo, bibere, bibi, bibitus *v* **(3rd)** drink; toast; visit, frequent (w, river name); drain, draw off; thirst for; suck;

binus, bina, binum *adi* two by two; 2 each; in pairs; 2 at time; on 2 occasions; double, twofold;

birrum, birri *n* **(2nd)** *n* cloak (wool, silk) to keep off rain;

blandimentum, blandimenti *n* **(2nd)** *n* blandishment, coaxing, wheedling behaviour, cajolery; favours; charm, delight;

bonus, bona -um, melior -or -us, optimus -a -um *adi* good, honest, brave, noble, kind, pleasant, right, useful; valid; healthy;

bos, bovis *n* **(3rd)** *c* ox; bull; cow; ox-ray; cattle (pl.); (ox-like animals); [luca ~ =>

elephant];

brachium, brachi(i) *n* **(2nd)** *n* arm; lower arm, forearm; claw; branch, shoot; earthwork connecting forts;

brevis, breve, brevior -or -us, brevissimus -a -um *adi* short, little, small, stunted; brief, concise, quick; narrow, shallow; humble;

breviter, brevitius, brevitissime *adv* shortly, briefly, in a nut shell; quickly; for, within a short distance, time;

brumalis, brumalis, brumale *adi* wintry; during winter; connected with winter solstice, winter;

bubalus, bubali *n* **(2nd)** *m* antelope, gazelle; wild ox, buffalo;

cadaver, cadaveris *n* **(3rd)** *n* corpse, cadaver, dead body; ruined city;

cado, cadere, cecidi, casus *v* **(3rd)** *intrans* fall, sink, drop, plummet, topple; be slain, die; end, cease, abate; decay;

caelum, caeli *n* **(2nd)** *n* heaven, sky, heavens; space; air, climate, weather; universe, world; Jehovah;

caesus, caesus *n* **(4th)** *m* cutting, cutting off;

calcar, calcaris *n* **(3rd)** *n* spur (for horse); spur, incitement, stimulus; spur of a cock;

calculus, calculi *n* **(2nd)** *m* pebble; (bladder) stone; piece for reckoning, voting, game; calculation; counter; small weight; live coal (Def);

calor, caloris *n* **(3rd)** *m* heat; warmth, glow; warm, hot, summer heat, weather; fever; passion, zeal; love;

campus, campi *n* **(2nd)** *m* plain; level field, surface; open space for battle, games; sea; scope; campus;

candidus, candida -um, candidior -or -us, candidissimus -a -um *adi* bright, clear, transparent; clean, spotless; lucid; candid; kind; innocent, pure; radiant, unclouded; (dressed in) white; of light colour; fair skinned, pale;

capillus, capilli *n* **(2nd)** *m* hair; hair of head; single hair; hair, fur, wool of animals; hair-like fiber;

capio, capere, additional, forms *v* *trans* take hold, seize; grasp; take bribe; arrest, capture; put on; occupy; captivate;

captivus, captiva, captivum *adi* caught, taken captive; captured (in war), imprisoned; conquered; of captives;

captus, capta, captum *adi* captured,

captive;

caput, capitis *n* **(3rd)** *n* head; person; life; leader; top; source, mouth (river); capital (punishment); heading; chapter, principal division; [~ super pedibus => head over heels];

careo, carere, carui, caritus *v* **(2nd)** be without, absent from, devoid of, free from; miss; abstain from, lack, lose;

carnis, carnis *n* **(3rd)** *f* meat, flesh; the_body; pulp, flesh of plants, sapwood; soft part; low passions;

carpo, carpere, carpsi, carptus *v* **(3rd)** *trans* seize, pick, pluck, gather, browse, tear off; graze, crop; tease, pull out, card (wool); separate, divide, tear down; carve; despoil, fleece; pursue, harry; consume, erode;

castellum, castelli *n* **(2nd)** *n* redoubt, fortress, stronghold, fortified settlement, refuge; castle, citadel; castle, reservoir (where water from aqueduct is collected for distribution); town, village; (mediaeval);

casteria, casteriae *n* **(1st)** *f* part of a ship?; (where rowers were accustomed to rest, rower's room *l+s*);

castitas, castitatis *n* **(3rd)** *f* chastity, fidelity; virginity; sexual, moral, ritual purity; integrity, morality;

castrum, castri *n* **(2nd)** *n* fort, fortress; camp (pl.), military camp, field; army; war service; day's march; castle, fortress; (fortified) town; [~ doloris => catafalque, coffin platform];

castus, casta -um, castior -or -us, castissimus -a -um *adi* pure, moral; chaste, virtuous, pious; sacred; spotless; free from, untouched by;

catholicus, catholica, catholicum *adi* catholic; universal; (Roman) Catholic, orthodox;

catholicus, catholici *n* **(2nd)** *c* Catholic, one baptized and fully in communion with Catholic Church;

catulus, catuli *n* **(2nd)** *m* young dog, puppy, whelp; dog (any age); young of any animal, pup, cub; fetter;

causa, causae *n* **(1st)** *f* cause, reason, motive; origin, source, derivation; responsibility, blame; symptom; occasion, subject; plea, position; lawsuit, case, trial; proviso, stipulation; thing(s); [sine causa => in vain (Vulgate)];

cavallus, cavalli *n* **(2nd)** *m* horse; cavalry;

celebratus, celebrata, celebratum *adi* crowded, much frequented, festive; current, popular; celebrated, distinguished;

celebris, celebris, celebre *adi* famous, celebrated, renowned; honoured, distinguished; famed; notorious; oft repeated, frequent; busy, crowded, much used, frequented, populous; festive;

celo, celare, celavi, celatus *v* **(1st)** *trans* conceal, hide, keep secret; disguise; keep in dark, in ignorance; shield;

celsus, celsa, celsum *adi* high, lofty, tall; haughty; arrogant, proud; prominent, elevated; erect; noble;

centenarium, centenarii *n* **(2nd)** *n* hundred (Roman) pounds weight, hundredweight;

centenarius, centenaria, centenarium *adi* containing, consisting of, numbering, having, costing hundred; hundred; hundredfold;

centum, centesimus -a -um, centeni -ae -a, centie(n)s *num* one hundred;

cerebrum, cerebri *n* **(2nd)** *n* brain; top of the head, skull; bud; seat of senses, intelligence; anger, wrath;

cerno, cernere, crevi, cretus *v* **(3rd)** *trans* sift, separate, distinguish, discern, resolve, determine; see; examine; decide;

certamen, certaminis *n* **(3rd)** *n* contest, competition; battle, combat, struggle; rivalry; (matter in) dispute;

certe *adv* surely, certainly, without doubt, really; at least, any rate, in all events;

certus, certa -um, certior -or -us, certissimus -a -um *adi* fixed, settled, firm; certain; trusty, reliable; sure; resolved, determined;

cervix, cervicis *n* **(3rd)** *f* neck (sg, pl.), nape; severed neck, head; cervix, neck (bladder, uterus, jar, land);

ceterum *adv* moreover; but yet; still, for the rest, but, besides; in other respects;

chartularius, chartularii *n* **(2nd)** *m* court archivist, keeper of archives (of court); Best read here as ruler of Ravenna;

chorus, chori *n* **(2nd)** *m* chorus; choral passage in a play; dancing, singing performance, ers; school; round, ring dance; dancers; movement of planets; magistrate's court; multitude; choir; singing; sanctuary; those in sanctuary;

Christianus, Christiani *n* **(2nd)** *m* Christian, follower of Christ; Christian clergyman; Christianity (pl.);

cibarium, cibari(i) *n* **(2nd)** *n* ration, allowance of food (pl.); food, provisions; food for animals, feed, fodder;

cibus, cibi *n* **(2nd)** *m* food; fare, rations; nutriment, sustenance, fuel; eating, a meal; bait;

cimelium, cimelii *n* **(1st)** *n* treasure;

circa *adv* around, all around; round about; near, in vicinity, company; on either side;

circa *prep acc* around, on bounds of; about, near (space, time, numeral); concerning; with;

circuitus, circuitus *n* **(4th)** *m* going round; patrol, circuit; way, path round; circumference; outer surface, edge; revolution, spinning, rotation; (recurring) cycle; period; circumlocution;

circumdo, circumdare, circumdedi, circumdatus *v* **(1st)** *trans* surround; envelop, post, put, place, build around; enclose; beset; pass around;

circumseptus, circumsepta, circumseptum *adi* fenced, hedged in, enclosed, walled in; surrounded, encircled;

cisterna, cisternae *n* **(1st)** *f* cistern; underground, sunken tank, reservoir for water; (or wine *l+s*); ditch, pit;

cito, citius, citissime *adv* quickly, fast, speedily, with speed; soon, before long; readily; easily;

civis, civis *n* **(3rd)** *c* fellow citizen; countryman, woman; citizen, free person; a Roman

civitas, civitatis *n* **(3rd)** *f* community, city, town, state; citizens; citizen rights, citizenship; naturalization;

clades, cladis *n* **(3rd)** *f* defeat, reverse; casualties, slaughter, carnage, devastation; ruins; dissolution; disaster, ruin, calamity; plague; pest, bane, scourge (cause of disaster);

clareo, clarere, -, - *v* **(2nd)** *intrans* shine bright, clearly; be clear, plain, understandable, obvious; be famous, renowned;

clarus, clara -um, clarior -or -us, clarissimus -a -um *adi* clear, bright, gleaming; loud, distinct; evident, plain; illustrious, famous;

classis, classis *n* **(3rd)** *f* class, division of Romans; grade (pupils); levy, draft; fleet, navy; group, band;

claudo, claudere, clausi, clausus *v* **(3rd)** *intrans* limp, stumble, falter, hesitate; be weak, imperfect, fall short; be lame, hobble;

clerus, cleri *n* **(2nd)** *m* clergy, clerical order;

coapto, coaptare, coaptavi, coaptatus *v* **(1st)** *trans* fit, join, adjust together; make by joining;

coepio, coepere, coepi, coeptus *v* **(3rd)** begin, commence, initiate; set foot on; (usu. *perf passive* w, *passive* INF; *pres* early);

cognomen, cognominis *n* **(3rd)** *n* surname, family, 3rd name; name (additional, derived from a characteristic);

cogo, cogere, coegi, coactus *v* **(3rd)** *trans* collect, gather, round up, restrict, confine; force, compel; convene; congeal;

colligo, colligere, collegi, collectus *v* **(3rd)** *trans* collect, assemble, bring, gather, hold, keep together; combine; harvest; pick up; obtain, acquire, amass; rally; recover; sum up; deduce, infer; compute, add up;

color, coloris *n* **(3rd)** *m* colour; pigment; shade, tinge; complexion; outward appearance, show; excuse, pretext

coma, comae *n* **(1st)** *f* hair, hair of head, mane of animal; wool, fleece; foliage, leaves; rays;

comes, comitis *n* **(3rd)** *c* comrade, companion, associate, partner; soldier, devotee, follower of another;

cometa, cometae *n* **(1st)** *f* comet; meteor; luminous body in sky w, trail, tail; (portent of disaster);

commeatus, commeatus *n* **(4th)** *m* supplies, provisions; goods; voyage; passage; convoy, caravan; furlough, leave;

commendo, commendare, commendavi, commendatus *v* **(1st)** *trans* entrust, give in trust; commit; recommend, commend to; point out, designate;

committo, committere, commisi, commissus *v* **(3rd)** bring together, unite, join, connect, attach; put together, construct; entrust; engage (battle), set against; begin, start; bring about; commit; incur; forfeit;

commotus, commotus *n* **(4th)** *m* movement; moving, agitation;

commune, communis *n* **(3rd)** *n* joint,

common, public property, rights; public; public places, interests (pl.); common feature, characteristic, general rule, terms; general; common lot, remedy;

compello, compellere, compuli, compulsus *v* (3rd) *trans* drive together (cattle), round up; force, compel, impel, drive; squeeze; gnash;

competenter, competentius, competentissime *adv* suitably, appositely; properly, becomingly;

compono, componere, composui, compositus *v* (3rd) *trans* compare; place, put, add, collect together, collate; match (up); store, hoard; calm; construct, build; arrange, compile, compose, make up; organize, order; settle;

comprehendo, comprehendere, comprehendi, comprehensus *v* (3rd) *trans* catch, seize, grasp firmly; arrest; take hold, root, fire, ignite; conceive (baby); embrace; include, cover, deal with (in speech, law); express (by term, symbol);

compresse, compressius, compressissime *adv* briefly, succinctly, in a compressed manner; urgently, pressingly, insistently;

compulso, compulsare, compulsavi, compulsatus *v* (1st) *trans* batter, pound;

concido, concidere, concidi, - *v* (3rd) *intrans* fall down, faint, dead, victim, to earth, short, collapse; drop, subside; decline; perish, be slain, sacrificed; lose one's case, fail, give out, lose heart, decay;

concido, concidere, concidi, concisus *v* (3rd) *trans* cut, chop up, down, to pieces; crop; ruin, kill, destroy; divide minutely; beat;

concipio, concipere, concepi, conceptus *v* (3rd) *trans* take in, up, receive, catch; derive, draw (from); contain, hold; grasp; adopt; wed; form, devise; understand, imagine; conceive, be mother of; utter (oath, prayer);

concremo, concremare, concremavi, concrematus *v* (1st) *trans* consume by fire; burn up, down entirely, completely, thoroughly; burn together;

concubo, concubare, concubavi, concubatus *v* (1st) *dat* lie with (sexual and not); have sexual intercourse with;

conculco, conculcare, conculcavi, conculcatus *v* (1st) *trans* tread, trample upon, underfoot, down; crush, oppress; despise, disregard;

concupio, concupere, concupivi, concupitus *v* (3rd) *trans* desire, wish greatly, eagerly, ardently; covet, long for, be desirous of;

concurro, concurrere, concucurri, concursus *v* (3rd) *intrans* run, assemble, knock, snap together; agree, fit, concur; coincide; make same claim; charge, fight, engage in battle; come running up, in large numbers; rally;

condo, condere, condidi, conditus *v* (3rd) *trans* put, insert (into); store up, put away, preserve, bottle (wine); bury, inter; sink; build, found, make; shut (eyes); conceal, hide, keep safe; put together, compose; restore; sheathe (sword); plunge, bury (weapon in enemy); put out of sight;

condono, condonare, condonavi, condonatus *v* (1st) *trans* give (away, up); present; make present of; forgive, pardon, absolve; sacrifice to;

confero, conferre, contuli, collatus *v trans* bring together, carry, convey; collect, gather, compare; unite, add; direct, aim; discuss, debate, confer; oppose; pit, match against another; blame; bestow, assign;

configo, configere, confixi, confixus *v* (3rd) *trans* fasten, nail together, construct; set, cover with studs, points; drive in (nails); ierce through, transfix; strike down, pierce with a weapon;

confugio, confugere, confugi, confugitus *v* (3rd) *intrans* flee (for refuge, safety, protection); take refuge; have recourse, appeal to;

congero, congerere, congessi, congestus *v* (3rd) *trans* collect, bring, get together, amass; heap, pile up, on; build, construct; compile; consign (to one's stomach); assemble, crowd together; give repeatedly, shower;

congero, congeronis *n* (3rd) *m* thief;

congredior, congredi, congressus sum *v* (3rd) *dep* meet, approach, near; join in battle, come to grips; contend, engage (at law);

congrego, congregare, congregavi, congregatus *v* (1st) *trans* collect, bring together, assemble, convene; flock, congregate; group; concentrate;

coniugo, coniugare, coniugavi, coniugatus *v* **(1st)** *trans* join in marriage; form a friendship; join together, unite in;

coniunx, coniugis *n* **(3rd)** *c* spouse, mate, consort; husband, wife, bride, fiancee, intended; concubine; yokemate;

conlactaneus, conlactanei *n* **(2nd)** *m* foster-brother; one nourished at the same breast;

conligo, conligere, conlegi, conlectus *v* **(3rd)** *trans* collect, assemble, bring, gather, hold, keep together; combine; harvest; pick up; obtain, acquire, amass; rally; recover; sum up; deduce, infer; compute, add up;

conloco, conlocare, conlocavi, conlocatus *v* **(1st)** *trans* place, put, set in order, proper position, arrange; station, post, position; apply; ut together, assemble; settle, establish in a place, marriage; billet; lie down;

conor, conari, conatus sum *v* **(1st)** *dep* attempt, try, endeavour, make an effort; exert oneself; try to go, rise, speak;

conperio, conperire, conperi, conpertus *v* **(4th)** *trans* learn, discover, find (by investigation); verify, know for certain; find guilty;

conperior, conperiri, conpertus sum *v* **(4th)** *dep* learn, discover, find (by investigation); verify, know for certain; find guilty;

conpesco, conpescere, conpescui, - *v* **(3rd)** *trans* restrain, check; quench; curb, confine, imprison; hold in check; block, close;

conquiro, conquirere, conquisivi, conquisitus *v* **(3rd)** *trans* seek out; hunt, rake up; investigate; collect; search out, down, for diligently;

consanguineus, consanguinei *n* **(2nd)** *c* kinsman, blood relation; brother (M); a sister (F); kindred, relations (pl.);

conscius, consci(i) *n* **(2nd)** *c* accomplice, accessory; partner; confidante; one privy to (crime, plot); witness;

conscius, conscia, conscium *adi* conscious, aware of, knowing, privy (to); sharing (secret) knowledge; guilty;

conscriptus, conscripti *n* **(2nd)** *m* senator, counselor; enrolling of the people for the purpose of bribery;

consensus, consensus *n* **(4th)** *m* agreement (opinion), consent, harmony; unanimity; conclusion, plot, conspiracy; general

consensus; custom; combined action; [concensu => by general consent];

consentio, consentire, consensi, consensus *v* **(4th)** join, share in sensation, feeling; be in agreement, harmony; be of the same mind; act together; plot, conspire, combine; coincide; be in conjunction (planets); agree, consent; fit, be consistent, in sympathy, unison with; favour; assent to;

conservo, conservare, conservavi, conservatus *v* **(1st)** keep safe, intact, save (from danger); preserve, maintain; spare; keep, observe;

consilium, consili(i) *n* **(2nd)** *n* debate, discussion, deliberation, consultation; advice, counsel, suggestion; adviser; decision, resolution; intention, purpose, policy, plan, action; diplomacy, strategy; deliberative, advisory body; state council, senate; jury; board of assessors; intelligence, sense, capacity for judgment, invention; mental ability; choice;

conspicio, conspicere, conspexi, conspectus *v* **(3rd)** *trans* observe, see, witness; notice; watch; gaze, stare on; catch, be in sight of; face; have appearance; attract attention; discern; (*passive*) be conspicuous, visible;

constitutio, constitutionis *n* **(3rd)** *f* constitution, disposition, structure, character; arrangement, organization, system; ordinance, decree, decision; position, ordering; destiny; definition of a term;

constitutus, constituta, constitutum *adi* constituted, disposed, endowed with a nature; ordered, arranged, appointed; being;

consto, constare, constiti, constatus *v* **(1st)** *intrans* agree, correspond, fit, be correct; be dependent, based upon; exist, continue, last; be certain, decided, consistent, sure, fixed, established, well-known, apparent, plain; stand firm, still, erect, together; remain motionless, constant; consist of, in;

construo, construere, construxi, constructus *v* **(3rd)** *trans* heap, pile, load (up); make, build, construct; arrange (in group); amass, collect;

consueo, consuere, consuevi, consuetus *v* **(2nd)** *trans* accustom; become accustomed; be accustomed, inure, habituate. familiarize;

consuetudo, consuetudinis *n* **(3rd)** *f* habit,

custom, usage, way; normal, general, customary practice, tradition, convention; experience; empirical knowledge; sexual, illicit intercourse, intimacy, affair;

consul, consulis *n* **(3rd)** *m* consul (highest elected Roman official - 2, year); supreme magistrate elsewhere;

consurgo, consurgere, consurrexi, consurrectus *v* **(3rd)** *intrans* rise, stand up (body of people); rise (jury, from meal, to speak, from bed); ambush; aspire to, rouse, prepare; break out, come from hiding; grow, spring up, rise;

contamino, contaminare, contaminavi, contaminatus *v* **(1st)** *trans* corrupt, defile (w, filth, intercourse), stain, befoul spoil; ruin, dishonour; debase w, mixture of inferior material; contaminate, infect; pollute (morally);

contemplor, contemplari, contemplatus sum *v* **(1st)** *dep* observe, note, notice, gaze, look hard at, regard; contemplate, consider carefully;

contempno, contempnere, contempsi, contemptus *v* **(3rd)** *trans* think little of; look down on, take poor view of; pay no heed, disregard, slight; treat with, hold in contempt, scorn, disdain; despise; keep away from, avoid;

contemptor, contemptoris *n* **(3rd)** *m* despiser; one who looks down on, scorns; who disregards, pays no heed (to life);

contextus, contexta, contextum *adi* interwoven; closely joined; connected, coherent (literary composition); continuous, uninterrupted, unbroken; covered with a network (of rivers);

contingo, contingere, contigi, contactus *v* **(3rd)** *intrans* happen, befall, turn out, come to pass, be granted to one; be produced;

contingo, contingere, contigi, contactus *v* **(3rd)** *trans* touch; reach (to); border on, be connected with; affect, hit; take hold, seize; colour, stain; lay hands on, appropriate; smite; affect emotionally, move, touch;

continue *adv* continuously; without interruption;

contra *adv* facing, face-to-face, in the eyes; towards, up to; across; in opposite direction; against, opposite, opposed, hostile, contrary, in reply to; directly over, level; otherwise, differently; conversely; on the contrary; vice versa;

contra *prep acc* against, facing, opposite; weighed against; as against; in resistance, reply to; contrary to, not in conformance with; the reverse of; otherwise than; towards, up to, in direction of; directly over, level with; to detriment of;

contrarius, contraria, contrarium *adi* opposite, contrary, in contradiction; antithetical; opposed, hostile, adverse; incompatible; reversed, inverted; reciprocal, mutual; counterbalancing;

contrarius, contrarii *n* **(2nd)** *m* opponent, adversary; antagonist;

contribuo, contribuere, contribui, contributus *v* **(3rd)** *trans* unite, incorporate, join, attach (to state); assign, allot; contribute, give, share;

conveho, convehere, convexi, convectus *v* **(3rd)** *trans* bring, carry, bear together, to one place; collect, gather; get in (harvest);

converto, convertere, converti, conversus *v* **(3rd)** turn upside down, side-to-side; invert, transpose, convulse; turn over (soil), dig; turn backwards, recoil; retort; drive back, repulse; direct (course, attention); translate; modify, adapt; change, alter, transform; convert (to cash), pay over; cause to turn, revolve, rotate; turn, wheel about; reverse; shift, transfer;

convivium, convivi(i) *n* **(2nd)** *n* banquet, feast, dinner party; guests, people at party; dining-club; living together

copia, copiae *n* **(1st)** *f* plenty, abundance, supply; troops (pl.), supplies; forces; resources; wealth; number, amount, quantity; sum, whole amount; means, opportunity; access, admission; copy;

copiosus, copiosa -um, copiosior -or -us, copiosissimus -a -um *adi* plentiful, copious, abundant; well supplied, equipped, w, ample resources; prolific; eloquent, w, plentiful command of the language; verbose; rich, wealthy; fruitful;

cor, cordis *n* **(3rd)** *n* heart; mind, soul, spirit; intellect, judgment; sweetheart; souls, persons (pl.);

coris, coris (coridos) n **(3rd)** *f* a plant; seed of a plant.

corpus, corporis *n* **(3rd)** *n* body; person, self; virility; flesh; corpse; trunk; frame(work); collection, sum; substantial, material, concrete object, body; particle, atom; corporation, guild;

corrigia, corrigiae *n* **(1st)** *f* shoe-lace, tie, thong for securing shoes to feet; thong of any kind;

corripio, corripere, corripui, correptus *v* **(3rd)** *trans* seize, grasp, snatch up, lay hold of; sweep off; carry away; appropriate, arrogate; censure, reproach, rebuke, chastise; shorten, abridge; hasten (upon); catch (fire);

corrumpo, corrumpere, corrupi, corruptus *v* **(3rd)** *trans* spoil, rot; taint, contaminate; damage, ruin, undo; destroy, deface; digest; infect; ervert, corrupt, deprave; bribe, suborn; seduce, tempt, beguile; falsify;

corruo, corruere, corrui, corrutus *v* **(3rd)** fall, break down, fall to ground, from height, collapse; be ruined, come to grief; topple (house, wall), totter; subside (ground); rush, sweep together; overthrow;

corruptio, corruptionis *n* **(3rd)** *f* corruption; bribery, seduction from loyalty; diseased, corrupt condition;

coruscatio, coruscationis *n* **(3rd)** *f* flash, gleam; glittering;

corusco, coruscare, coruscavi, coruscatus *v* **(1st)** brandish, shake, quiver; flash, glitter, emit, reflect intermittent, quivering light;

cottidie *adv* daily, every day; day by day; usually, ordinarily, commonly;

credo, credere, credidi, creditus *v* **(3rd)** trust, entrust; commit, consign; believe, trust in, rely on, confide; suppose; lend (money) to, make loans, give credit; believe, think, accept as true, be sure;

crinis, crinis *n* **(3rd)** *m* hair; lock of hair, tress, plait; plume (helmet); tail of a comet;

crudelis, crudele, crudelior -or -us, crudelissimus -a -um *adi* cruel, hardhearted, unmerciful, severe, bloodthirsty, savage, inhuman; harsh, bitter;

crudus, cruda -um, crudior -or -us, crudissimus -a -um *adi* raw; bloody, bleeding; crude, cruel, rough, merciless; fierce, savage; grievous; youthful, hardy, vigourous; fresh, green, immature; undigested; w, undigested food;

crux, crucis *n* **(3rd)** *f* cross; hanging tree; impaling stake; crucifixion; torture, torment, trouble, misery

cubo, cubare, cubui, cubitus *v* **(1st)** *intrans* lie (down, asleep); recline, incline; lie, be in bed, rest, sleep; be sick, dead;

cultus, cultus *n* **(4th)** *m* habitation; cultivation (land); civilization, refinement; polish, elegance; care, worship, devotion, observance; form of worship, cult; training, education; ersonal care, maintenance, grooming; style; finery, splendor; neatness, order;

cum *adv* when, at the time, on each occasion, in the situation that; after; since, although; as soon; while, as (well as); whereas, in that, seeing that; on, during which;

cum *prep abl* with, together, jointly, along, simultaneous with, amid; supporting; attached; under command, at the head of; having, containing, including; using, by means of;

cuncta, cunctae *n* **(1st)** *f* all (pl.) (F); all with a stated, implied exception;

cunctus, cuncta, cunctum *adi* altogether (usu. pl.), in a body; every, all, entire; total, complete; whole of;

cupiditas, cupiditatis *n* **(3rd)** *f* enthusiasm, eagerness, passion; (carnal) desire; lust; greed, usury, fraud; ambition

cupio, cupere, cupivi, cupitus *v* **(3rd)** *trans* wish, long, be eager for; desire, want, covet; desire as a lover; favour, wish well;

cupo, cuponis *n* **(3rd)** *m* shopkeeper, salesman, huckster; innkeeper, keeper of a tavern;

curriculum, curriculi *n* **(2nd)** *n* act of running; race; lap, track; chariot; course of action, heavenly bodies;

curro, currere, cucurri, cursus *v* **(3rd)** *intrans* run, trot, gallop, hurry, hasten, speed, move, travel, proceed, flow swiftly, quickly;

dactylus, dactyli *n* **(2nd)** *m* dactyl (metrical foot long-short-short); long (finger-like) grape, date, mollusk;

damno, damnare, damnavi, damnatus *v* **(1st)** *trans* pass, pronounce judgment, find guilty; deliver, condemn, sentence; harm, damn, doom; discredit; seek, secure condemnation of; find fault; bind, oblige under a will;

datio, dationis *n* **(3rd)** *f* giving, assigning, allotting, handing over (act); transfer;

donation, gift; payment;

datum, dati *n* **(2nd)** *n* present, gift; that which is given; debit; [~ dandis => w, all supplied];

de *prep abl* down, away from, from, off; about, of, concerning; according to; with regard to;

deambulo, deambulare, deambulavi, deambulatus *v* **(1st)** *intrans* take a walk, go for a walk; walk abroad; walk much; promenade;

debeo, debere, debui, debitus *v* **(2nd)** owe; be indebted, responsible for, obliged, bound, destined; ought, must, should;

debilis, debile, debilior -or -us, debilissimus -a -um *adi* weak, feeble, frail; crippled, disabled; wanting, deprived (competence); ineffective

decedo, decedere, decessi, decessus *v* **(3rd)** *intrans* withdraw, retire, go off, away, depart, leave; relinquish, cease; desert, abandon; quit office and return home; make, get out of the way; yield; wane; fall short; stray, digress; pass away, depart life, die; subside, cease (feelings); disappear;

decem, decimus -a -um, deni -ae -a, decie(n)s *num* ten; (ten men);

decima, decimae *n* **(1st)** *f* tithe; tenth part; (offering, tax, largesse); tax, right to collect 10%; 10th hour;

deditus, dedita -um, deditior -or -us, deditissimus -a -um *adi* devoted, attached to, fond of; devoted, directed, given over (to) (activity);

dedo, dedere, dedidi, deditus *v* **(3rd)** *trans* give up, in, surrender; abandon, consign, devote (to); yield, hand, deliver over;

deduco, deducere, deduxi, deductus *v* **(3rd)** *trans* lead, draw, pull, bring, stretch down, away, out, off; escort; eject, evict (claimant); divert, draw (water); draw (sword); spin; deduct, reduce, lessen; describe; deduce launch, bring downstream (ship); remove (force); entice; found, settle (colony);

defendo, defendere, defendi, defensus *v* **(3rd)** *trans* defend, guard, protect, look after; act, speak, plead, write for defense; prosecute; repel, fend, ward off, avert, prevent; support, preserve, maintain; defend (right);

defensio, defensionis *n* **(3rd)** *f* defense, protection; act of defending; argument, justification in defense, excuse; legal maintenance of a right; legal prosecution, punishment;

defero, deferre, detuli, delatus *v* carry, bring, sink, fall down, off; convey, deliver, transfer; reduce, slope (down to); flow, carry, run down (to sea); pay, remit; deposit, record, register; bear, produce; bring, lodge information (about), report; indict, accuse, denounce; defer (to); offer; bestow upon, confer, award, grant, entrust; submit, refer for decision; honour; export (mediaeval usage);

deficio, deficere, defeci, defectus *v* **(3rd)** *intrans* fail, falter; run short, out; grow weak, faint; come to end; revolt, rebel, defect; ass away; become extinct, die, fade out; subside, sink; suffer eclipse, wane;

defico, deficare, deficavi, deficatus *v* **(1st)** *trans* strain, clear, cleanse, remove dregs, impurities from; defecate; set at ease;

defunctus, defuncti *n* **(2nd)** *c* dead person; (usu. male); the dead (pl.);

dehinc *adv* hereafter, henceforth, from here, now on; afterwards; for, in the future, next; then, after that, thereupon; at a later stage; for the rest; next (in order);

deicio, deicere, deieci, deiectus *v* **(3rd)** *trans* throw, pour, jump, send, put, push, force, knock, bring down; cause to fall, drop; hang; overthrow, bring down, depose; kill, destroy; shoot, strike down; fell (victim); unhorse; let fall; shed; purge, evacuate bowel; dislodge, rout; drive, throw out;

deinceps *adv* in order, succession, turn; one after, beside another, successively; etc; very next

deinde *adv* then, next, afterward; thereon, henceforth, from there, then; in next position, place;

deleo, delere, delevi, deletus *v* **(2nd)** *trans* erase, wipe, scratch, remove (letters, marks), wipe, blot out, expunge, delete; annihilate, exterminate, kill every member of a group; put end to, end, abolish; destroy completely, demolish, obliterate, crush; ruin; overthrow; nullify, annul;

delibero, deliberare, deliberavi, deliberatus *v* **(1st)** weigh, consider, deliberate, consult (oracle); ponder, think over; resolve, decide on

delibo, delibare, delibavi, delibatus *v* **(1st)** skim, flake, scrape off; channel off (water); pick out a choice specimen; perform; diminish, detract (from); take away a little as to render imperfect; infringe; take a little, wear away, nibble at; taste (of), touch on (subject) lightly;

delicatus, delicata -um, delicatior -or -us, delicatissimus -a -um *adi* luxurious, sumptuous, addicted to pleasure; self-indulgent, comfortable; pampered; foppish, effeminate; polite, elegant; charming; tender; voluptuous; wanton; skittish, frisky, frivolous; fastidious, squeamish; delicate, dainty, pretty, fine;

deligo, deligare, deligavi, deligatus *v* **(1st)** *trans* bind fast, tie (up), fasten; make fast by tying; bandage; tie (bandage);

demolio, demolire, demolivi, demolitus *v* **(4th)** *trans* throw, cast off, remove; pull, tear down, demolish, destroy, lay waste; abolish;

demon, demonis *n* **(3rd)** *m* spirit, supernatural being, intermediary between man and god; evil demon, devil;

demorior, demori, demortuus sum *v* **(3rd)** *dep* die; die off, out (group, class), become extinct; be gone; long for much (w, *acc*);

demoror, demorari, demoratus sum *v* **(1st)** *dep* detain, cause delay, keep waiting, back, hold up; keep (from); delay, linger, stay;

denique *adv* finally, in the end; and then; at worst; in short, to sum up; in fact, indeed;

depasco, depascere, depavi, depastus *v* **(3rd)** *trans* graze, feed, pasture (cattle); devour, eat up; waste, consume (w, fire); lay waste;

depello, depellere, depuli, depulsus *v* **(3rd)** drive, push out, off, away, aside, repel; expel; remove, wean; banish utterly; dislodge; avert; rebut; veer away; force to withdraw, desist; turn out, dismiss;

depingo, depingere, depinxi, depictus *v* **(3rd)** *trans* paint, depict, portray; describe; decorate, colour w, paint; embroider;

depono, deponere, deposivi, depositus *v* **(3rd)** *trans* put, lay down, aside, away; let drop, fall; give up; resign; deposit, entrust, commit; lift off; take off (clothes); have (hair, beard, nails) cut; shed (tusks); ull down, demolish; plant (seedlings); set up, place; lay to rest; fire;

depopulo, depopulare, depopulavi, depopulatus *v* **(1st)** *trans* sack, plunder, pillage, rob, despoil; ravage, devastate, destroy, lay waste; overgraze;

deporto, deportare, deportavi, deportatus *v* **(1st)** bring, convey (to); carry along, down (current); transport; take, bring home;

deprecor, deprecari, deprecatus sum *v* **(1st)** *dep* avert by prayer; entreat, pray, beg; intercede, beg pardon, mercy, relief, exemption;

deque *adv* downwards;

derelinquo, derelinquere, dereliqui, derelictus *v* **(3rd)** *trans* leave behind, abandon, discard; forsake, desert; neglect; leave derelict; bequeath;

describo, describere, descripsi, descriptus *v* **(3rd)** *trans* describe, draw, mark, trace out; copy, transcribe, write; establish (law, right)

desero, deserere, deserui, desertus *v* **(3rd)** *trans* leave, depart, quit, desert; forsake, abandon, give up; withdraw support, let down; cease to be concerned with; fail, fall short; (*passive* w, *abl*) be without, deprived;

despecto, despectare, despectavi, despectatus *v* **(1st)** *trans* look over, down at, survey; overlook; rise above, overtop; despise, look down on;

despero, desperare, desperavi, desperatus *v* **(1st)** despair (of); have no, give up hope (of, that); give up as hopeless (of cure);

destruo, destruere, destruxi, destructus *v* **(3rd)** *trans* demolish, pull, tear down; destroy, ruin; demolish, refute (arguments, evidence);

desum, deesse, defui, defuturus *v* be wanting, lacking; fail, miss; abandon, desert, neglect; be away, absent, missing;

detrunco, detruncare, detruncavi, detruncatus *v* **(1st)** *trans* mutilate, cut pieces from; lop off, cut off; remove branches from; maim; behead;

Deus, Dei *n* **(2nd)** *m* God (Christian text); god; divine essence, being, supreme being; statue of god;

devasto, devastare, devastavi, devastatus *v* **(1st)** *trans* devastate, lay waste (territory, people); ravage; slaughter;

devenio, devenire, deveni, deventus *v* **(4th)** *intrans* come to, arrive, turn up (at); go (to see, stay); reach; land; turn to; extend to;

devinco, devincere, devici, devictus *v*

(3rd) *trans* subdue; defeat decisively, conquer, overcome entirely;

diaconus, diaconi *n* **(2nd)** *m* deacon; cleric of minor orders (first, highest level);

dico, dicere, dixi, dictus *v* **(3rd)** say, declare, state; allege, declare positively; assert; plead (case); talk, speak; make speech; play (instrument); pronounce, articulate; utter; mean; name, call; appoint, fix, set (date); designate, declare intention of giving;

dies, diei *n* **(5th)** *c* day; daylight; (sunlit hours); (24 hours from midnight); open sky; weather; specific day; day in question; date of letter; festival; lifetime, age; time;

dignitas, dignitatis *n* **(3rd)** *f* worth, excellence; fitness, suitability (for task),; honour, esteem, standing; rank, status; merit; dignity; position, authority, office; dignitaries (pl.);

dignus, digna -um, dignior -or -us, dignissimus -a -um *adi* appropriate, suitable; worthy, deserving, meriting; worth (w, *abl, gen*);

digredior, digredi, digressus sum *v* **(3rd)** *dep* depart; come, go away; part, separate, deviate; divorce; G:digress, leave (topic);

dilabor, dilabi, dilapsus sum *v* **(3rd)** *dep* run, flow, slip away, spread (liquids); dissolve, melt away, disperse (clouds); fall apart, to pieces; disintegrate; break down (body), collapse, decay, perish; flee, escape; scatter, fall into confusion; be lost; go to ruin; pass (time);

diluvium, diluvi(i) *n* **(2nd)** *n* flood, inundation; deluge; destruction (by water);

dimitto, dimittere, dimisi, dimissus *v* **(3rd)** *trans* send away, off; allow to go, let go, off; disband, discharge, dismiss (soldiers); dissolve (assembly); part with; put away; divorce; pay off, settle (debt); release, set free; allow to escape, slip away; shake off, scatter, shed; discontinue, renounce, abandon, forsake, forgo, give up (activity); dispatch;

direptio, direptionis *n* **(3rd)** *f* plundering, pillage, sacking; struggle for share; scramble; stealing; rape;

dirigo, dirigere, direxi, directus *v* **(3rd)** *trans* arrange, set in line, direction; align; set in order; form up, fall in (army); mark, fix (boundary); demarcate; straighten (out); level; square (up); oint; direct (word, attention); bring proceedings; end word w, inflection; direct (course, steps), turn, steer, guide; propel, direct (missiles, blows);

diripio, diripere, diripui, direptus *v* **(3rd)** *trans* pull, tear apart, to pieces, away; tear asunder, to shreds; pull out, off; divert; grab; scramble for; snatch a share of; strive; run after, compete for (favour); lunder, pillage, spoil, lay waste; seize and divide; steal, rob; distress;

dirum, diri *n* **(2nd)** *n* fearful things; ill-boding events;

dirus, dira -um, dirior -or -us, dirissimus -a -um *adi* awful, dire, dreadful (omen); ominous, frightful, terrible, horrible; skillful;

discedo, discedere, discessi, discessus *v* **(3rd)** go, march off, depart, withdraw; scatter, dissipate; abandon; lay down (arms);

discooperio, discooperire, discooperui, discoopertus *v* **(4th)** *trans* expose, bare, lay bare, uncover; disclose; put, take off, remove;

discrimen, discriminis *n* **(3rd)** *n* crisis, separating line, division; distinction, difference;

discurro, discurrere, discucurri, discursus *v* **(3rd)** *intrans* run off in different directions; run, dash around, about; wander; roam;

dispar, (gen.), disparis *adi* unequal, disparate, unlike;

dispareo, disparere, disparui, disparitus *v* **(2nd)** *intrans* disappear, vanish, vanish out of sight;

disrumpo, disrumpere, disrupi, disruptus *v* **(3rd)** *trans* cause to break apart, off, shatter, burst, split, disrupt, sever; (*passive*) get broken;

dissipo, dissipare, dissipavi, dissipatus *v* **(1st)** scatter, disperse, dissipate, squander; destroy completely; circulate;

dissonantia, dissonantiae *n* **(1st)** *f* dissonance; discrepancy;

distraho, distrahere, distraxi, distractus *v* **(3rd)** draw, pull, tear apart, wrench, separate, (sub)divide; sell in parcels; distract;

diurnus, diurna, diurnum *adi* by day, of the day; daily;

diuturnus, diuturna -um, diuturnior -or -

us, diuturnissimus -a -um *adi* lasting, lasting long;

diversus, diversa, diversum *adi* opposite; separate, apart; diverse, unlike, different; hostile;

dives, divitis (gen.), divitior -or -us, divitissimus -a -um *adi* rich, wealthy; costly; fertile, productive (land); talented, well endowed;

divido, dividere, divisi, divisus *v* (3rd) divide; separate, break up; share, distribute; distinguish;

divinitas, divinitatis *n* (3rd) *f* divinity, quality, nature of God; divine excellence, power, being; divining;

divinitus *adv* from heaven, by a god, by divine influence, inspiration; divinely, admirable;

divinus, divina -um, divinior -or -us, divinissimus -a -um *adi* divine, of a deity, god, godlike; sacred; divinely inspired, prophetic; natural;

do, dare, dedi, datus *v* (1st) *trans* give; dedicate; sell; pay; grant, bestow, impart, offer, lend; devote; allow; make; surrender, give over; send to die; ascribe, attribute; give birth, produce; utter;

dolo, dolare, dolavi, dolatus *v* (1st) *trans* hew, chop into shape, fashion, devise; inflict blows, batter, cudgel soundly, drub;

dolor, doloris *n* (3rd) *m* pain, anguish, grief, sorrow, suffering; resentment, indignation;

domesticus, domestici *n* (2nd) *m* household member;

Dominica, Dominicae *n* (1st) *f* Sunday, the Lord's day;

dominus, domini *n* (2nd) *m* owner, lord, master; the Lord; title for ecclesiastics, gentlemen;

domnus, domni *n* (2nd) *m* lord, master; the Lord; ecclesiastic, gentleman; (shortened form of dominus);

dormio, dormire, dormivi, dormitus *v* (4th) *intrans* sleep, rest; be, fall asleep; behave as if asleep; be idle, do nothing;

dorsum *adv* down, downwards, beneath, below; (motion, direction, order); in lower situation;

dotatus, dotata, dotatum *adi* richly endowed;

draco, draconis *n* (3rd) *m* dragon; snake;

ducatus, ducatus *n* (4th) *m* leadership; position, function of a leader; generalship;

duco, ducere, duxi, ductus *v* (3rd) lead, command; think, consider, regard; prolong;

dum *coni* while, as long as, until; provided that;

duodecim, duodecimus -a -um, duodeni -ae -a, duodecie(n)s *num* twelve;

durum, duri *n* (2nd) *n* hardships (pl.);

durus, dura -um, durior -or -us, durissimus -a -um *adi* hard, stern; harsh, rough, vigorous; cruel, unfeeling, inflexible; durable;

e, ex *prep* *abl* out of, from; by reason of; according to; because of, as a result of;

ecce *interi* behold! see! look! there! here! [ecce eum => here he is];

ecclesia, ecclesiae *n* (1st) *f* church; assembly, meeting of the assembly;

eclipsis, eclipsis *n* (3rd) *f* eclipse;

econtra *adv* the_contrary; the_reverse;

edico, edicere, edixi, edictus *v* (3rd) proclaim, declare; appoint;

educo, educare, educavi, educatus *v* (1st) bring up; train; educate; rear;

efficio, efficere, effeci, effectus *v* (3rd) bring about; effect, execute, cause; accomplish; make, produce; prove;

effodio, effodere, effodi, effossus *v* (3rd) dig out, excavate; gouge out;

effusio, effusionis *n* (3rd) *f* outpouring, shedding; profusion, lavishness, extravagance, excess;

effusus, effusa -um, effusior -or -us, effusissimus -a -um *adi* vast, wide, sprawling; disheveled, loose (hair, reins); disorderly; extravagant;

egredior, egredi, egressus sum *v* (3rd) *dep* go, march, come out; set sail; land, disembark; surpass, go beyond;

eiicio, eiicere, eieci, eiectus *v* (3rd) *trans* cast, throw, fling, drive out, up, extract, expel, discharge, vomit; out (tongue);

elabor, elabi, elapsus sum *v* (3rd) *dep* slip away; escape; elapse;

elatio, elationis *n* (3rd) *f* glorification, extolling, lifting; (ceremonial) carrying out; ecstasy; exaltation;

elegans, (gen.), elegantis *adi* elegant, fine, handsome; tasteful; fastidious, critical; discriminating, polite;

elemosina, elemosinae *n* (1st) *f* alms,

almshouse; gift to a church, religious foundation; pity; (act of) mercy;

elevo, elevare, elevavi, elevatus *v* **(1st)** lift up, raise; alleviate; lessen; make light of;

eligo, eligere, elegi, electus *v* **(3rd)** pick out, choose;

eloquor, eloqui, elocutus sum *v* **(3rd)** *dep* speak out, utter;

enim *coni* namely (postpos.); indeed; in fact; for; I mean, for instance, that is to say;

enimvero *coni* to be sure, certainly; well, upon by word; but, on the other hand; what is more;

enitor, eniti, enixus sum *v* **(3rd)** *dep* bring forth, bear, give birth to; struggle upwards, mount, climb, strive;

eo, ire, ivi(ii), itus *v* go, walk; march, advance; pass; flow; pass (time); ride; sail;

equitatus, equitatus *n* **(4th)** *m* cavalry, horse-soldiers; equestrian order; bodies of cavalry (pl.); horsemanship, equitation, riding; creature in heat (mare);

equus, equi *n* **(2nd)** *m* horse; steed;

erga *prep acc* towards, opposite (friendly);

ergo *adv* therefore; well, then, now;

erogatio, erogationis *n* **(3rd)** *f* paying out, distribution;

erogo, erogare, erogavi, erogatus *v* **(1st)** pay out, expend;

error, erroris *n* **(3rd)** *m* wandering; error; winding, maze; uncertainty; deception;

ethimologia, ethimologiae *n* **(1st)** *f* etymology;

etiam *coni* and also, besides, furthermore, in addition, as well; even, actually; yes, indeed; now too, as yet, still, even now; yet again; likewise; (particle); (et-iam);

eunuchus, eunuchi *n* **(2nd)** *m* eunuch;

evacuo, evacuare, evacuavi, evacuatus *v* **(1st)** *trans* empty (vessel); purge, evacuate (bowels);

evado, evadere, evasi, evasus *v* **(3rd)** evade, escape; avoid;

evagino, evaginare, evaginavi, evaginatus *v* **(1st)** *trans* unsheathe;

evangelista, evangelistae *n* **(1st)** *m* preacher (of the Gospel); evangelist;

evolvo, evolvere, evolvi, evolutus *v* **(3rd)** roll out, unroll; disclose, unfold; extricate; pursue; explain;

exagito, exagitare, exagitavi, exagitatus *v* **(1st)** drive out; stir up, disturb continually, harass; attack, scold, discuss;

exametrus, exametra, exametrum *adi* hexameter; with six metrical feet; (of verse);

exardesco, exardescere, exarsi, exarsus *v* **(3rd)** *intrans* flare, blaze up; break out; glow; rage; be provoked, enraged; be exasperated;

excello, excellere, -, excelsus *v* **(3rd)** be eminent, preeminent; excel;

exclamo, exclamare, exclamavi, exclamatus *v* **(1st)** exclaim, shout; cry out, call out;

excludo, excludere, exclusi, exclusus *v* **(3rd)** shut out, shut off; remove; exclude; hinder, prevent;

excresco, excrescere, excrevi, excretus *v* **(3rd)** grow out or up; grow up; grow;

execratio, execrationis *n* **(3rd)** *f* imprecation, curse;

exemplum, exempli *n* **(2nd)** *n* example, sample, specimen; instance; precedent, case; warning, deterrent; attern, model; parallel, analogy; archetype; copy, reproduction, transcription;

exenium *adv* by mistake;

exeo, exire, exivi(ii), exitus *v intrans* come, go, sail, march, move out, forth, away, leave; pass (away), expire, perish, die; discharge (fluid); rise (river); become visible; issue, emerge, escape; sprout;

exercitus, exercitus *n* **(4th)** *m* army, infantry; swarm, flock;

exhibeo, exhibere, exhibui, exhibitus *v* **(2nd)** present; furnish; exhibit; produce;

exigo, exigere, exegi, exactus *v* **(3rd)** drive out, expel; finish; examine, weigh;

exiguus, exigua, exiguum *adi* small; meager; dreary; a little, a bit of; scanty, petty, short, poor;

exilio, exilire, exilivi, - *v* **(4th)** *intrans* spring, leap, burst forth, out, leap up, start up, bound; emerge into existence;

eximo, eximere, exemi, exemptus *v* **(3rd)** *trans* remove, extract, take, lift out, off, away; banish, get rid of; free, save, release;

exinde *adv* thence; after that, next in order, thereafter, then; furthermore; by that cause;

existo, existere, existiti, existitus *v* **(3rd)** step forth, appear; arise; become; prove to be; be;

exorior, exoriri, exortus sum *v* **(4th)** *dep* come out, come forth; bring; appear; rise, begin, spring up; cheer up;

expecto, expectare, expectavi, expectatus *v* **(1st)** await, expect; anticipate; hope for;

expedio, expedire, expedivi, expeditus *v* **(4th)** disengage, loose, set free; be expedient; procure, obtain, make ready;

expergiscor, expergisci, experrectus sum *v* **(3rd)** *dep* awake; bestir oneself;

expertus, experta, expertum *adi* well-proved, tested; shown to be true;

expeto, expetere, expeti, expetitus *v* **(3rd)** ask for; desire; aspire to; demand; happen; fall on

expleo, explere, explevi, expletus *v* **(2nd)** fill out; fill, fill up, complete, finish; satisfy, satiate;

expolio, expoliare, expoliavi, expoliatus *v* **(1st)** plunder;

expugno, expugnare, expugnavi, expugnatus *v* **(1st)** assault, storm; conquer, plunder; accomplish; persuade;

exsequor, exsequi, exsecutus sum *v* **(3rd)** *dep* follow, go along, on with; pursue for vengeance, punishment; strive, search after; ersist in; execute, carry out; rehearse; attain, arrive at, accomplish;

exsto, exstare, -, - *v* **(1st)** stand forth, out; exist; be extant, visible; be on record;

extendo, extendere, extendi, extensus *v* **(3rd)** *trans* stretch, thrust out; make taut; extend, prolong, continue; enlarge, increase; make even, straight, smooth; stretch out in death, (*passive*) lie full length;

extinguo, extinguere, extinxi, extinctus *v* **(3rd)** quench, extinguish; kill; destroy;

extra *adv* outside;

extra *prep acc* outside of, beyond, without, beside; except;

extremum, extremi *n* **(2nd)** *n* limit, outside; end;

exul, exulis *n* **(3rd)** *c* exile (M, F), banished person; wanderer;

fabula, fabulae *n* **(1st)** *f* story, tale, fable; play, drama; [fabulae! => rubbish!, nonsense!];

facies, faciei *n* **(5th)** *f* shape, face, look; presence, appearance; beauty; achievement;

facile, facilius, facillime *adv* easily, readily, without difficulty; generally, often; willingly; heedlessly;

facio, facere, feci, factus *v* **(3rd)** *trans* make, build, construct, create, cause, do;

have built, made; fashion; work (metal); act, take action, be active; (bowels); act, work (things), function, be effective; roduce; produce by growth; bring forth (young); create, bring into existence; compose, write; classify; provide; do, perform; commit crime; suppose, imagine;

fallaciter, fallacius, fallicissime *adv* deceptively, deceitfully, with intent to deceive; falsely, in misleading manner;

fallo, fallere, fefelli, falsus *v* **(3rd)** deceive; slip by; disappoint; be mistaken, beguile, drive away; fail; cheat;

fames, famis *n* **(3rd)** *f* hunger; famine; want; craving;

famosus, famosa -um, famosior -or -us, famosissimus -a -um *adi* famous, noted, renowned; talked of; infamous, notorious; slanderous, libelous;

fanum, fani *n* **(2nd)** *n* sanctuary, temple;

faretra, faretrae *n* **(1st)** *f* quiver;

fascia, fasciae *n* **(1st)** *f* band, strip; ribbon; B:bandage; streak, band of cloud; headband, filet; sash (Ecc);

fateor, fateri, fassus sum *v* **(2nd)** *dep* admit, confess (w, *acc*); disclose; acknowledge; praise (w, *dat*);

faveo, favere, favi, fautus *v* **(2nd)** favour (w, *dat*), befriend, support, back up;

febris, febris *n* **(3rd)** *f* fever, attack of fever;

feliciter *adv* happily;

femina, feminae *n* **(1st)** *f* woman; female;

fenestra, fenestrae *n* **(1st)** *f* window, opening for light; loophole, breach; orifice; inlet; opportunity;

feodalis, feodalis *n* **(3rd)** *m* vassal;

ferax, feracis (gen.), feracior -or -us, feracissimus -a -um *adi* fruitful, fertile. prolific;

ferox, (gen.), ferocis *adi* wild, bold; warlike; cruel; defiant, arrogant;

ferreus, ferrea, ferreum *adi* iron, made of iron; cruel, unyielding; (blue);

ferrum, ferri *n* **(2nd)** *n* iron; any tool of iron; weapon, sword;

ferus, fera, ferum *adi* wild, savage; uncivilized; untamed; fierce;

fervor, fervoris *n* **(3rd)** *m* heat, boiling heat; boiling, fermenting; ardor, passion, fury; intoxication;

festivitas, festivitatis *n* **(3rd)** *f* festivity, feast; conviviality, charm; heart's delight;

humour (speaker), wit;

festus, festa, festum *adi* festive, joyous; holiday; feast day; merry; solemn;

fideliter, fidelius, fidelissime *adv* faithfully, constantly, loyally; earnestly; reliably, accurately; securely, firmly; with reliance on God;

fides, fidei *n* **(5th)** *f* faith, loyalty; honesty; credit; confidence, trust, belief; good faith;

fiducia, fiduciae *n* **(1st)** *f* trust, confidence; faith, reliance; courage;

fidus, fida, fidum *adi* faithful, loyal; trusting, confident;

filia, filiae *n* **(1st)** *f* daughter;

finio, finire, finivi, finitus *v* **(4th)** limit, end; finish; determine, define; mark out the boundaries;

finis, finis *n* **(3rd)** *c* boundary, end, limit, goal; (pl.) country, territory, land;

fio, feri, factus sum *v* *semidep* happen, come about; result (from); take place, be held, occur, arise (event); be made, created, instituted, elected, appointed, given; be prepared, done; develop; be made, become; (facio *passive*); [fiat => so be it, very well; it is being done];

fiscus, fisci *n* **(2nd)** *m* money-bag, purse; imperial exchequer;

flamma, flammae *n* **(1st)** *f* flame, blaze; ardor, fire of love; object of love;

fletus, fletus *n* **(4th)** *m* weeping, crying, tears; wailing; lamenting;

floreo, florere, florui, - *v* **(2nd)** flourish, blossom, be prosperous; be in one's prime;

flumen, fluminis *n* **(3rd)** *n* river, stream; any flowing fluid; flood; onrush; [adverso ~ => against current];

fluo, fluere, fluxi, fluxus *v* **(3rd)** flow, stream; emanate, proceed from; fall gradually;

fluvius, fluvi(i) *n* **(2nd)** *m* river, stream; running water;

fodio, fodere, fodi, fossus *v* **(3rd)** dig, dig out, up; stab;

foederatus, foederata, foederatum *adi* allied; treaty bound to Rome); federated; leagued together, confederated;

foedo, foedare, foedavi, foedatus *v* **(1st)** *trans* defile; pollute; soil, stain, make filthy, unclean; contaminate; corrupt; disgrace, dishonour; bring shame, discredit; sully, besmirch (person, reputation); disfigure, mar, spoil appearance, brightness, clearness, purity of; darken, dim; make (punishment) horrible, barbarous; mangle, hack, mutilate, ravage (land);

foedus, foederis *n* **(3rd)** *n* treaty, league, formal agreement (between states), alliance; P:peace, amity; contract, compact; promise, undertaking; marriage bond; other sexual unions; bond, tie (friendship, kinship, hospitality); law, limit (imposed by nature, fate);

foetidus, foetida, foetidum *adi* stinking; foul-smelling; having a bad smell, odor;

foetor, foetoris *n* **(3rd)** *m* stench; bad, foul smell, stink; foulness, noisomeness;

foetus, foetus *n* **(4th)** *m* offspring, young (animals); children (of a parent); brood, litter; fetus, fetus, young while still in the womb; embryo (Cal); birth, bringing forth young; laying (egg); bearing young, breeding; conception; fruit of plant; produce, crop; offshoot, branch, sucker, sapling; bearing fruit;

folium, foli(i) *n* **(2nd)** *n* leaf;

forma, formae *n* **(1st)** *f* form, figure, appearance; beauty; mold, pattern;

fors, fortis *n* **(3rd)** *f* chance; luck, fortune; accident;

fortasse *adv* perhaps, possibly; it may be;

forte *adv* by chance; perhaps, perchance; as luck would have it;

fortis, forte, fortior -or -us, fortissimus -a -um *adi* strong, powerful, mighty, vigourous, firm, steadfast, courageous, brave, bold;

fortiter, fortius, fortissime *adv* strongly; bravely; boldly;

forum, fori *n* **(2nd)** *n* market; forum (in Rome); court of justice;

frater, fratris *n* **(3rd)** *m* brother; cousin;

frenus, freni *n* **(2nd)** *m* bridle, harness, rein, bit; harnessed horses, team; check, restraint, brake; mastery;

frequens, frequentis (gen.), frequentior -or -us, frequentissimus -a -um *adi* crowded; numerous, full, frequented, populous; repeated, frequent, constant;

frequenter *adv* often, frequently; in great numbers; in crowds;

frigor, frigoris *n* **(3rd)** *m* cold; chill (esp. of feverish person) (Souter);

frons, frontis *n* **(3rd)** *c* forehead, brow;

face; look; front; fore part of anything;

frumentum, frumenti *n* **(2nd)** *n* grain; crops;

frutectum, frutecti *n* **(2nd)** *n* thicket of shrubs, bushes, covert; shrubs, bushes (pl.);

fuga, fugae *n* **(1st)** *f* flight, fleeing, escape; avoidance; exile; fugue (music);

fugio, fugere, fugi, fugitus *v* **(3rd)** flee, fly, run away; avoid, shun; go into exile;

fugitivus, fugitiva, fugitivum *adi* fugitive;

fugo, fugare, fugavi, fugatus *v* **(1st)** put to flight, rout; chase away; drive into exile;

fulgens, fulgentis (gen.), fulgentior -or -us, fulgentissimus **-a** **-um** *adi* flashing, gleaming, glittering, resplendent; brilliant (white); bright, splendid;

fulmen, fulminis *n* **(3rd)** *n* lightning, flash; thunderbolt; crushing blow;

funditus *adv* utterly, completely, without exception; from the bottom, to the ground, by the root;

funus, funeris *n* **(3rd)** *n* burial, funeral; funeral rites; ruin; corpse; death;

furtum, furti *n* **(2nd)** *n* theft; trick, deception; stolen article;

gaudeo, gaudere, gavisus sum *v* **(2nd)** *semidep* be glad, rejoice;

gelida, gelidae *n* **(1st)** *f* ice cold water;

genealogia, genealogiae *n* **(1st)** *f* genealogy;

generalis, generalis, generale *adi* general, generic; shared by, common to a class, kind; of the nature of a thing;

generaliter *adv* generally, in general;

genetrix, genetricis *n* **(3rd)** *f* mother, ancestress;

genitor, genitoris *n* **(3rd)** *m* father; creator; originator;

genitus, genita, genitum *adi* begotten; engendered;

gens, gentis *n* **(3rd)** *f* tribe, clan; nation, people; Gentiles;

genu, genus *n* **(4th)** *n* knee;

germino, germinare, germinavi, germinatus *v* **(1st)** sprout forth;

gero, gerere, gessi, gestus *v* **(3rd)** bear, carry, wear; carry on; manage, govern; (se gerere = to conduct oneself);

gladius, gladi(i) *n* **(2nd)** *m* sword;

glans, glandis *n* **(3rd)** *f* mast, acorn, beechnut, chestnut; missile, bullet thrown, discharged from

grammatica, grammaticae *n* **(1st)** *f* grammar; philology;

gratanter *adv* with joy; with rejoicing;

gratia, gratiae *n* **(1st)** *f* popularity, esteem, credit (w, bona); partiality, favouritism; unpopularity (w, mala); favour, goodwill, kindness, friendship; influence; gratitude; thanks (pl.); Graces; agreeableness, charm; grace;

gravis, grave, gravior -or -us, gravissimus **-a** **-um** *adi* heavy; painful; important; serious; pregnant; grave, oppressive, burdensome;

gubernaculum, gubernaculi *n* **(2nd)** *n* helm, rudder, steering oar of ship; helm of "ship of state"; government;

habeo, habere, habui, habitus *v* **(2nd)** have, hold, consider, think, reason; manage, keep; spend, pass (time);

habitans, habitantis *n* **(3rd)** *c* inhabitant; dweller;

hasta, hastae *n* **(1st)** *f* spear, lance, javelin; spear stuck in ground for public auction, centumviral court;

haud *adv* not, not at all, by no means; not (as a particle);

heresis, heresis *n* **(3rd)** *f* philosophical, religious school of thought, sect; heresy, heretical doctrine;

hereticus, heretica, haereticum *adi* heretical, of, belonging to heretical religious doctrines;

heu *interi* oh! ah! alas! (an expression of dismay or pain);

hiemo, hiemare, hiemavi, hiematus *v* **(1st)** winter, pass the winter, keep winter quarters; be wintry, frozen, stormy;

hiems, hiemis *n* **(3rd)** *f* winter, winter time; rainy season; cold, frost; storm, stormy weather;

Hierosolymum, Hierosolymi *n* **(2nd)** *n* Jerusalem (pl.) (Hebrew);

hirtus, hirta, hirtum *adi* hairy, shaggy, covered with hair, wool; thick growth (plants); rough, unpolished;

hispidus, hispida, hispidum *adi* rough, shaggy, hairy; bristly; dirty;

Hister, Histri, *n* **(2nd)** *m* Danube

historia, historiae *n* **(1st)** *f* history; account; story;

hodie *adv* today, nowadays; at the present time;

homo, hominis *n* **(3rd)** *m* man, human being, person, fellow; [novus homo => nouveau riche];

honor, honoris *n* **(3rd)** *m* honour; respect, regard; mark of esteem, reward; dignity, grace; public office;

hora, horae *n* **(1st)** *f* hour; time; season; [Horae => Seasons];

hornus, horna, hornum *adi* this year's; born, produced in the current year;

hortor, hortari, hortatus sum *v* **(1st)** *dep* encourage; cheer; incite; urge; exhort;

hospes, (gen.), hospitis *adi* of relation between host and guest; that hosts; that guests; foreign, alien;

hostis, hostis *n* **(3rd)** *c* enemy (of the state); stranger, foreigner; the enemy (pl.);

huc *adv* here, to this place; to this point;

humanitas, humanitatis *n* **(3rd)** *f* human nature, character, feeling; kindness, courtesy; culture, civilization;

humanus, humana -um, humanior -or -us, humanissimus -a -um *adi* human; kind; humane, civilized, refined; [~ hostiae => human sacrifice];

iacio, iacere, ieci, iactus *v* **(3rd)** throw, hurl, cast; throw away; utter;

iam *adv* now, already, by, even now; besides; [non ~ => no longer; ~ pridem => long ago];

ibi *adv* there, in that place; thereupon;

icio, icere, ici, ictus *v* **(3rd)** hit, strike; smite, stab, sting; [foedus ~ => conclude, make a treaty, league];

ictus, ictus *n* **(4th)** *m* blow, stroke; musical, metrical beat; measure (music);

ideo *adv* therefore, for the reason that, for that reason;

ieiuno, ieiunare, ieiunavi, ieiunatus *v* **(1st)** *intrans* fast; abstain form;

igitur *coni* therefore (postpositive), so, then; consequently; accordingly; well, in that case;

igneus, ignea, igneum *adi* fiery, hot; ardent;

ignominia, ignominiae *n* **(1st)** *f* disgrace, ignominy, dishonour;

ignoro, ignorare, ignoravi, ignoratus *v* **(1st)** not know; be unfamiliar with; disregard; ignore; be ignorant of;

illac *adv* that way;

illic *adv* in that place, there, over there;

illuc *adv* there, thither, to that place, point;

imago, imaginis *n* **(3rd)** *f* likeness, image, appearance; statue; idea; echo; ghost, phantom;

immensum *adv* to an enormous extent, degree;

immineo, imminere, -, - *v* **(2nd)** threaten, be a threat (to); overhang, be imminent; with *dat*;

immuto, immutare, immutavi, immutatus *v* **(1st)** change, alter, transform;

imperator, imperatoris *n* **(3rd)** *m* emperor; general; ruler; commander (-in-chief);

imperialis, imperialis, imperiale *adi* imperial; of the (Roman) emperor;

imperium, imperi(i) *n* **(2nd)** *n* command; authority; rule, supreme power; the state, the empire;

impero, imperare, imperavi, imperatus *v* **(1st)** order, command, levy; rule (over) (w, *dat*);

impossibilis, impossibilis, impossibile *adi* impossible;

in *prep abl* in, on, at (space); in accordance with, regard to, the case of; within (time);

in *prep acc* into; about, in the mist of; according to, after (manner); for; to, among;

inaestimabilis, inaestimabilis, inaestimabile *adi* priceless, beyond all price; inestimable; not to be reckoned in money; undeserving of valuation (phil.); not to be judged, unaccountable; valueless;

inauditus, inaudita, inauditum *adi* unheard (of), novel, new;

incarnatio, incarnationis *n* **(3rd)** *f* incarnation, embodiment; union of divine and human in Christ;

incendium, incendi(i) *n* **(2nd)** *n* fire, conflagration; fiery heat; fiery passion, love, hostility; arson (Latham); incendiary missile; meteor; P:flames (pl.); [annonae ~ => high price of grain];

incendo, incendere, incendi, incensus *v* **(3rd)** *trans* set on fire; set fire to, kindle, burn; cause to flame, burn; keep fire burning; scorch; make fiery hot (fever, thirst); light up; cause to glow; intensify; inspire, fire, rouse, excite, inflame; provoke, incense, aggravate;

incertus, incerta, incertum *adi* uncertain; unsure, inconstant, variable; doubtful;

increpo, increpare, increpavi, increpatus *v* **(1st)** *intrans* rattle, snap, clash, roar, twang, make noise; (alarm, danger); strike noisily;

increpo, increpare, increpui, increpitus *v* **(1st)** *intrans* rattle, snap, clash, roar, twang, make noise; (alarm, danger); strike noisily;

incurro, incurrere, incucurri, incursus *v* **(3rd)** run into or towards, attack, invade; meet (with); befall;

incurvo, incurvare, incurvavi, incurvatus *v* **(1st)** make crooked or bent; cause to bend down;

inde *adv* thence, thenceforth; from that place, time, cause; thereupon;

indictio, indictionis *n* **(3rd)** *f* men forming a levy; valuation, value, price; indicating, setting, rating value;

indigne, indignius, indigissime *adv* undeservedly; unjustly; unworthily; unbecomingly; shamefully; outrageously; dishonourably; indignantly; [~ fero => be indignant at; resent, take ill];

indocilis, indocilis, indocile *adi* unteachable, ignorant;

indoctus, indocta, indoctum *adi* untaught; unlearned, ignorant, untrained;

indulgentia, indulgentiae *n* **(1st)** *f* leniency, concession, pardon; kindness, gentleness; favour bounty; indulging; indulgence, remission before God of temporal punishment for sin;

indumentum, indumenti *n* **(2nd)** *n* garment, robe; something put on; (mask, sauce);

ineo, inire, inivi(ii), initus *v* enter; undertake; begin; go in; enter upon; [consilium ~ => form a plan];

inertia, inertiae *n* **(1st)** *f* ignorance; inactivity; laziness, idleness, sloth;

inexpugnabilis, inexpugnabilis, inexpugnabile *adi* impregnable, unconquerable, invincible;

infans, infantis *n* **(3rd)** *c* infant; child;

infer, infera -um, inferior -or -us, infumus -a -um *adi* below, beneath, underneath; of hell; vile; lower, further down; lowest, last;

infero, inferre, intuli, illatus *v trans* bring, carry in, import; advance, bring, march, step, move foward; impel, urge; inflict, cause, inflict, impose, inspire (w, *dat*); [bellum inferre => make war on]; put, throw, thrust in, on, insert; bury, inter; pay; charge as expense; append;

infesto, infestare, infestavi, infestatus *v* **(1st)** *trans* vex (w, attacks), harass, molest; make unsafe, disturb; infest; damage, impair;

influo, influere, influxi, influxus *v* **(3rd)** flow into; flow;

infra *adv* below, on the under side, underneath; further along; on the south;

infra *prep acc* below, lower than; later than;

ingens, ingentis (gen.), ingentior -or -us, ingentissimus -a -um *adi* not natural, immoderate; huge, vast, enormous; mighty; remarkable, momentous;

ingredior, ingredi, ingressus sum *v* **(3rd)** *dep* advance, walk; enter, step, go into; undertake, begin;

ingruo, ingruere, ingrui, - *v* **(3rd)** advance threateningly; make an onslaught on; break in, come violently, force;

inguen, inguinis *n* **(3rd)** *n* groin; the sexual organs, privy parts;

inimicus, inimici *n* **(2nd)** *m* enemy (personal), foe;

iniquitas, iniquitatis *n* **(3rd)** *f* unfairness, inequality, unevenness (of terrain);

iniustus, iniusta, iniustum *adi* unjust, wrongful; severe, excessive; unsuitable;

inlaesus, inlaesa, inlaesum *adi* unhurt, uninjured;

inmeritus, inmerita, inmeritum *adi* undeserving; undeserved, unmerited;

innumerabilis, innumerabilis, innumerabile *adi* innumerable, countless, numberless; without number; immense;

inruo, inruere, inrui, inrutus *v* **(3rd)** rush, dash, run in, upon, headlong, attack, charge; throw self on; enter eagerly in;

insepultus, insepulta, insepultum *adi* unburied;

insequor, insequi, insecutus sum *v* **(3rd)** *dep* follow, come after; attack; overtake; pursue (hostile); come after (time);

insero, inserere, inserui, insertus *v* **(3rd)** plant, sow; graft on; put in, insert;

insidia, insidiae *n* **(1st)** *f* ambush, ambuscade (pl.); plot; treachery, treacherous attack, device; trap, snare;

inspiro, inspirare, inspiravi, inspiratus *v* **(1st)** inspire; excite, inflame; instill, implant; breathe into; blow upon, into;

institutum, instituti *n* **(2nd)** *n* custom, principle; decree; intention; arrangement;

institution; habit, plan;

insula, insulae *n* **(1st)** *f* island; apartment house;

insuper *adv* above, on top; in addition (to); over;

insuper *prep acc* above, on top; in addition (to); over;

intactus, intacta, intactum *adi* untouched, intact; untried; virgin;

intellectus, intellectus *n* **(4th)** *m* comprehension, understanding; recognition, discerning; intellect; meaning, sense;

intellego, intellegere, intellexi, intellectus *v* **(3rd)** understand; realize;

intentio, intentionis *n* **(3rd)** *f* stretch, extension; spasm; tautness, tension; straining, concentration; aim;

inter *prep acc* between, among; during; [inter se => to each other, mutually];

intercedo, intercedere, intercessi, intercessus *v* **(3rd)** intervene; intercede, interrupt; hinder; veto; exist, come between;

interemo, interemere, interemi, interemptus *v* **(3rd)** *trans* do away with; kill, cut off from life; extinguish; put an end to, destroy;

intereo, interire, interivi(ii), interitus *v* perish, die; be ruined; cease;

interfectio, interfectionis *n* **(3rd)** *f* slaughter; act of killing; fatal end of an illness (Souter);

interfector, interfectoris *n* **(3rd)** *m* killer, murderer; assassin; destroyer (Souter);

interficio, interficere, interfeci, interfectus *v* **(3rd)** kill; destroy;

interim *adv* meanwhile, in the meantime; at the same time; however, nevertheless;

interitus, interitus *n* **(4th)** *m* ruin; violent, untimely death, extinction; destruction, dissolution;

internicio, internicionis *n* **(3rd)** *f* slaughter, massacre; extermination, total destruction of life; cause of such;

intimo, intimare, intimavi, intimatus *v* **(1st)** tell, tell about, relate, narrate, recount, describe;

intolerabilis, intolerabilis, intolerabile *adi* unable to endure, impatient (of); insufferable;

intra *prep acc* within, inside; during; under;

intra, interius, intime *adv* within, inside, on the inside; during; under; fewer than;

introduco, introducere, introduxi, introductus *v* **(3rd)** introduce, bring, lead in;

introeo, introire, introivi(ii), introitus *v* enter, go in or into; invade;

inundatio, inundationis *n* **(3rd)** *f* flood;

inutilis, inutilis, inutile *adi* useless, unprofitable, inexpedient, disadvantageous; harmful, helpless;

invado, invadere, invasi, invasus *v* **(3rd)** enter, attempt; invade; take possession of; attack (with in +acc.);

invenio, invenire, inveni, inventus *v* **(4th)** come upon; discover, find; invent, contrive; reach, manage to get;

invideo, invidere, invidi, invisus *v* **(2nd)** envy, regard with envy, ill will; be jealous of; begrudge, refuse;

invidia, invidiae *n* **(1st)** *f* hate, hatred, dislike; envy, jealousy, spite, ill will; use of words, acts to arouse;

invisus, invisa, invisum *adi* hated, detested; hateful, hostile;

invito, invitare, invitavi, invitatus *v* **(1st)** invite, summon; challenge, incite; encourage; attract, allure, entice;

ita *adv* thus, so; therefore;

itaque *adv* and so, accordingly; thus, therefore, consequently;

itaque *coni* and so, therefore;

iter, itineris *n* **(3rd)** *n* journey; road; passage, path; march [route magnum => forced march];

iteratio, iterationis *n* **(3rd)** *f* repetition;

iubo, iubere, additional, forms *v* *trans* order, tell, command, direct; enjoin, command; decree, enact; request, ask, bid; pray;

iudex, iudicis *n* **(3rd)** *m* judge; juror;

iugo, iugare, iugavi, iugatus *v* **(1st)** marry; join (to);

iugum, iugi *n* **(2nd)** *n* yoke; team, pair (of horses); ridge (mountain), summit, chain;

iungo, iungere, iunxi, iunctus *v* **(3rd)** join, unite; bring together, clasp (hands); connect, yoke, harness;

iuramentum, iuramenti *n* **(2nd)** *n* oath;

ius, iuris *n* **(3rd)** *n* law; legal system; code; right; duty; justice; court; binding decision; oath;

iusiurandum, iusiurandi *n* **(2nd)** *n* oath;

iustus, iusta -um, iustior -or -us,

iustissimus -a -um *adi* just, fair, equitable; right, lawful, justified; regular, proper;

iuvenilis, iuvenilis, iuvenile *adi* youthful;

iuventus, iuventutis *n* **(3rd)** *f* youth; the age of youth (20-40), young persons; young men, knights;

iuxta *adv* nearly; near, close to, near by, hard by, by the side of; just as, equally;

iuxta *prep acc* near, (very) close to, next to; hard by, adjoining; on a par with; like;

Kalenda, Kalendae *n* **(1st)** *f* Kalends (pl.), 1st of month; *abb.* Kal., Kl.; day of proclamation, interest due;

laboro, laborare, laboravi, laboratus *v* **(1st)** work, labour; produce, take pains; be troubled, sick, oppressed, be in distress;

lacrima, lacrimae *n* **(1st)** *f* tear; exuded gum, sap; bit of lead; quicksilver from ore; weeping (pl.); dirge;

lactens, (gen.), lactentis *adi* suckling, unweaned; full of milk, sap, juicy; prepared with milk; milky white;

lacus, lacus *n* **(4th)** *m* basin, tank, tub; lake, pond; reservoir, cistern, basin, trough; lime-hole; bin; pit;

laesio, laesionis *n* **(3rd)** *f* injury, harm, hurt; part of speech to injure opponent's case (rhetoric), attack;

laetabundus, laetabunda, laetabundum *adi* greatly-rejoicing;

laetans, (gen.), laetantis *adi* rejoicing;

laetus, laeta -um, laetior -or -us, laetissimus -a -um *adi* happy, cheerful, joyful, glad; favourable, propitious; prosperous, successful; luxuriant, lush, rich, sleek; fertile (land); teeming, abounding; pleasing, welcome;

laicus, laica, laicum *adi* lay, common; of the laity, people; not priestly, in orders, consecrated;

lama, lamae *n* **(1st)** *f* bog, slough; llama;

lamento, lamentare, lamentavi, lamentatus *v* **(1st)** lament; utter cries of grief; bewail; lament for; complain that;

lana, lanae *n* **(1st)** *f* wool; fleece; soft hair; down; trifles;

lancea, lanceae *n* **(1st)** *f* lance; long light spear;

laqueus, laquei *n* **(2nd)** *m* noose; snare, trap;

large *adv* exceedingly;

largifluus, largiflua, largifluum *adi* flowing freely;

largior, largiri, largitus sum *v* **(4th)** *dep* grant; give bribes, presents corruptly; give generously, bountifully;

latebra, latebrae *n* **(1st)** *f* hiding place, retreat, lair; subterfuge;

latrocinium, latrocini(i) *n* **(2nd)** *n* brigandage, robbery, highway robbery; piracy, freebooting; villainy;

latus, lata -um, latior -or -us, latissimus -a -um *adi* wide, broad; spacious, extensive;

lavo, lavare, lavi, lavatus *v* **(1st)** wash, bathe; soak;

laxus, laxa -um, laxior -or -us, laxissimus -a -um *adi* wide, spacious, ample, roomy; loose, not close packed; slack, not tight; lax; unstrung; relaxed, at ease; unrestricted; breached, wide open; distant (time);

lea, leae *n* **(1st)** *f* lioness;

lectulus, lectuli *n* **(2nd)** *m* bed or couch;

legatus, legati *n* **(2nd)** *m* envoy, ambassador, legate; commander of a legion; officer; deputy;

legumen, leguminis *n* **(3rd)** *n* pulse, leguminous plant; pod-vegetable;

leo, leonis *n* **(3rd)** *m* lion;

levo, levare, levavi, levatus *v* **(1st)** *trans* lift, raise, hold up; support; erect, set up; lift off, remove (load); comfort; undo, take off; release, rid; free from (worry, expense); refresh, restore; lighten, lessen, relieve; reduce in force, potency; bring down (cost, prices); alleviate (condition); make smooth, polish; free from hair, depilate;

lex, legis *n* **(3rd)** *f* law; motion, bill, statute; principle; condition;

liber, libera -um, liberior -or -us, liberrimus -a -um *adi* free (man); unimpeded; void of; independent, outspoken, frank; free from tribute; unconstrained, unrestrained, unencumbered; licentious; idle; w, abandon;

liber, liberi *n* **(2nd)** *m* children (pl.); (sg. VOC) child;

liber, libri *n* **(2nd)** *m* book, volume; inner bark of a tree;

liberatio, liberationis *n* **(3rd)** *f* liberation, setting free, release, deliverance (from) (debt); acquittal, discharge;

libertas, libertatis *n* **(3rd)** *f* freedom, liberty; frankness of speech, outspokenness;

libido, libidinis *n* **(3rd)** *f* desire, longing,

wish, fancy; lust, wantonness; will, pleasure; passion, lusts (pl.);

ligneus, lignea, ligneum *adi* wooden, wood-; woody, like wood, tough, stringy; [soleae ~ => worn by parricide];

limen, liminis *n* **(3rd)** *n* threshold, entrance; lintel; house;

linea, lineae *n* **(1st)** *f* string, line (plumb, fishing); [alba ~ => white line at end of race course];

lingua, linguae *n* **(1st)** *f* tongue; speech, language; dialect;

litoralis, litoralis, litorale *adi* of the seashore;

littera, litterae *n* **(1st)** *f* letter (alphabet); (pl.) letter, epistle; literature, books, records, account;

litus, litoris *n* **(3rd)** *n* shore, seashore, coast, strand; river bank; beach, landing place;

loculus, loculi *n* **(2nd)** *m* spot, little, small place; compartment, pigeon-hole; coffin, bier (Vulgate); compartmented box (pl.), money-box; school satchel, case for writing material;

locus, loci *n* **(2nd)** *m* place, territory, locality, neighbourhood, region; position, point; aim point; site;

locusta, locustae *n* **(1st)** *f* locust; crustacean, lobster (w, marina, maris);

longe, longius, longissime *adv* far (off), distant, a long way; by far; for a long while, far (in future, past);

longitudo, longitudinis *n* **(3rd)** *f* length; longitude;

longus, longa -um, longior -or -us, longissimus -a -um *adi* long; tall; tedious, taking long time; boundless; far; of specific length, time;

loquor, loqui, locutus sum *v* **(3rd)** *dep* speak, tell; talk; mention; say, utter; phrase;

luctus, luctus *n* **(4th)** *m* grief, sorrow, lamentation, mourning; cause of grief;

luna, lunae *n* **(1st)** *f* moon; month;

lupus, lupi *n* **(2nd)** *m* wolf; grappling iron;

lux, lucis *n* **(3rd)** *f* light, daylight, light of day; life; world; day; [prima luce => at daybreak];

machina, machinae *n* **(1st)** *f* machine; siege engine; scheme;

magis *adv* to greater extent, more nearly; rather, instead; more; (forms COMP w, DJ);

magister, magistri *n* **(2nd)** *m* teacher, tutor, master, expert, chief; pilot of a ship; rabbi;

magistratus, magistratus *n* **(4th)** *m* magistracy, civil office; office; magistrate, functionary;

magnus, magna -um, maior -or -us, maximus -a -um *adi* large, great, big, vast, huge; much; powerful; tall, long, broad; extensive, spacious; great (achievement); mighty; distinguished; skilled; bold, confident; proud; full, complete, utter, pure; intense; loud; at high price; notable, famous; old;

male, peius, pessime *adv* badly, ill, wrongly, wickedly, unfortunately; extremely;

malignitas, malignitatis *n* **(3rd)** *f* ill-will, spite, malice; niggardliness;

malitia, malitiae *n* **(1st)** *f* ill will, malice; wickedness; vice, fault;

malus, mala -um, peior -or -us, - *adi* bad, evil, wicked; ugly; unlucky;

mamma, mammae *n* **(1st)** *f* breast, udder;

mandatum, mandati *n* **(2nd)** *n* order, command, commission; mandate; commandment;

mando, mandare, mandavi, mandatus *v* **(1st)** entrust, commit to one's charge, deliver over; commission; order, command;

mando, mandere, mandi, mansus *v* **(3rd)** chew, champ, masticate, gnaw; eat, devour; lay waste;

mane *adv* in the morning; early in the morning;

maneo, manere, mansi, mansus *v* **(2nd)** remain, stay, abide; wait for; continue, endure, last; spend the night (sexual);

manifesto *adv* undeniably, red-handed, in the act; evidently, plainly, manifestly;

mansues, (gen.), mansuetis *adi* tame; mild, gentle; soft; tamed;

manus, manus *n* **(4th)** *f* hand, fist; team; gang, band of soldiers; handwriting; (elephant's) trunk;

mare, maris *n* **(3rd)** *n* sea; sea water;

maritus, mariti *n* **(2nd)** *m* husband, married man; lover; mate;

marmor, marmoris *n* **(3rd)** *n* marble, block of marble, marble monument, statue; surface of the sea;

martyr, martyris *n c* martyr; witness; one who by his death bears witness to the truth of Christ;

mater, matris *n* **(3rd)** *f* mother, foster mother; lady, matron; origin, source, motherland, mother city;

matrimonium, matrimoni(i) *n* **(2nd)** *n* marriage; matrimony;

maturitas, maturitatis *n* **(3rd)** *f* ripeness;

maximus, maxima, maximum *adi* greatest, biggest, largest; longest; oldest; highest, utmost; leading, chief;

maxume *adv* especially, chiefly; certainly; most, very much; (forms SUPER w, *adj*, ADV);

medietas, medietatis *n* **(3rd)** *f* center, mid point, part; half; intermediate course, state; fact of being in middle;

mediocris, mediocris, mediocre *adi* medium, average, intermediate; middling, fair, ordinary, moderate, tolerable; trivial; commonplace; undistinguished; of humble station; mediocre; fairly small; minor;

memini, meminisse, - *v perfdef* remember (*perf* form, *pres* force); keep in mind, pay heed to; be sure; recall;

memor, (gen.), memoris *adi* remembering; mindful (of w, *gen*), grateful; unforgetting, commemorative;

mensa, mensae *n* **(1st)** *f* table; course, meal; banker's counter;

mensis, mensis *n* **(3rd)** *m* month;

mereo, merere, merui, meritus *v* **(2nd)** earn; deserve, merit, have right; win, gain, incur; earn soldier, whore pay, serve;

meretrix, meretricis *n* **(3rd)** *f* courtesan, kept woman; public prostitute; harlot;

meridianus, meridiani *n* **(2nd)** *m* meridian (geography);

meridies, meridiei *n* **(5th)** *m* noon; midday; south;

merito *adv* deservedly; rightly;

messor, messoris *n* **(3rd)** *m* reaper, harvester;

metuo, metuere, metui, - *v* **(3rd)** fear; be afraid; stand in fear of; be apprehensive, dread;

metus, metus *n* **(4th)** *m* fear, anxiety; dread, awe; object of awe, dread;

micans, (gen.), micantis *adi* flashing, gleaming, sparkling, twinkling, glittering;

miles, militis *n* **(3rd)** *m* soldier; foot soldier; soldiery; knight (Latham); knight's fee, service;

miliarium, miliari(i) *n* **(2nd)** *n* milestone, column resembling a milestone, the one at the Forum; a Roman mile;

mille, milis *n* **(3rd)** *n* thousand; thousands (men, things); miles; [~ passuum => thousand paces = 1 mile];

mina, minae *n* **(1st)** *f* threats (pl.), menaces; warning signs, evil omens, prognostications; pinnacles;

ministro, ministrare, ministravi, ministratus *v* **(1st)** *dat* attend (to), serve, furnish; supply;

minor, minari, minatus sum *v* **(1st)** *dep* threaten, speak, act menacingly; make threatening movement; give indication of;

mirabile, mirabilis *n* **(3rd)** *n* miracle; wondrous deed; wonders (pl. Ecc); wonderful things; marvelous works;

miraculum, miraculi *n* **(2nd)** *n* wonder, marvel; miracle, amazing act, event, object, sight; amazement; freak;

miror, mirari, miratus sum *v* **(1st)** *dep* be amazed, surprised, bewildered (at); look in wonder, awe, admiration at; admire, revere; wonder; marvel at;

mirus, mira, mirum *adi* wonderful, strange, remarkable, amazing, surprising, extraordinary;

miser, misera -um, miserior -or -us, miserrimus -a -um *adi* poor, miserable, wretched, unfortunate, unhappy, distressing;

miseria, miseriae *n* **(1st)** *f* misery, distress, woe, wretchedness, suffering;

misericordia, misericordiae *n* **(1st)** *f* pity, sympathy; compassion, mercy; pathos;

mitto, mittere, misi, missus *v* **(3rd)** send, throw, hurl, cast; let out, release, dismiss; disregard;

modo *adv* only, merely; just now, recently, lately; presently;

monachus, monachi *n* **(2nd)** *m* monk;

mons, montis *n* **(3rd)** *m* mountain; huge rock; towering heap;

mora, morae *n* **(1st)** *f* delay, hindrance, obstacle; pause;

morbus, morbi *n* **(2nd)** *m* sickness, illness, weakness; disease; distemper; distress; vice;

mors, mortis *n* **(3rd)** *f* death; corpse; annihilation;

mortalitas, mortalitatis *n* **(3rd)** *f* mortality; death;

mortuus, mortui *n* **(2nd)** *m* corpse, the dead one; the dead;

motus, motus *n* (4th) *m* movement, motion; riot, commotion, disturbance; gesture; emotion;

mox *adv* soon, next (time, position);

mulier, mulieris *n* (3rd) *f* woman; wife; mistress;

muliercula, mulierculae *n* (1st) *f* little, weak, foolish woman; little hussy;

multimodus, multimoda, multimodum *adi* various, manifold;

multitudo, multitudinis *n* (3rd) *f* multitude, great number; crowd; rabble, mob;

multus, multa -um, -, plurimus -a -um *adi* much, many, great, many a; large, intense, assiduous; tedious;

munio, munire, munivi, munitus *v* (4th) fortify; strengthen; protect, defend, safeguard; build (road);

munus, muneris *n* (3rd) *n* service; duty, office, function; gift; tribute, offering; bribes (pl.);

murmur, murmuris *n* (3rd) *n* murmur, mutter; whisper, rustle, hum, buzz; low noise; roar, growl, grunt, rumble;

murus, muri *n* (2nd) *m* wall, city wall;

mutuus, mutua, mutuum *adi* borrowed, lent; mutual, in return;

nam *coni* for, on the other hand; for instance;

namque *coni* for and in fact, on the other hand; insomuch as (strengthened nam);

narro, narrare, narravi, narratus *v* (1st) tell, tell about, relate, narrate, recount, describe;

nascor, nasci, natus sum *v* (3rd) *dep* be produced spontaneously, come into existence, being; spring forth, grow; live; be born, begotten, formed, destined; rise (stars), dawn; start, originate; arise;

navis, navis *n* (3rd) *f* ship; [navis longa => galley, battleship; ~ oneraria => transport, cargo ship];

nec *coni* nor, and..not; not..either, not even;

necesse, undeclined *adi* necessary, essential; unavoidable, compulsory, inevitable; a natural law; true;

neco, necare, necavi, necatus *v* (1st) *trans* kill, murder; put to death; suppress, destroy; kill (plant); quench, drown (fire);

nefarium, nefarii *n* (2nd) *n* crime; wicked, impious, nefarious, heinous act;

nefas, undeclined *n* N sin, violation of divine law, impious act; [fas et nefas => right and wrong];

nepos, nepotis *n* (3rd) *c* grandson, daughter; descendant; spendthrift, prodigal, playboy; secondary shoot;

neque *coni* nor [neque..neque=>neither..nor; neque solum..sed etiam=>not only..but also];

nescio, nescire, nescivi, nescitus *v* (4th) not know (how); be ignorant, unfamiliar, unaware, unacquainted, unable, unwilling;

nihil, undeclined *n* N nothing; no; trifle, thing not worth mentioning; nonentity; nonsense; no concern;

nihilominus *adv* never, none the less, notwithstanding, just the same; likewise, as well;

nimius, nimia, nimium *adi* excessive, too great;

nisi *coni* if not; except, unless;

nivalis, nivalis, nivale *adi* snowy, snow-covered; snow-like;

nobilis, nobile, nobilior -or -us, nobilissimus -a -um *adi* noble, well born; aristocratic; outstanding (in rank, deed); important, prominent; famous, celebrated; well, generally known; remarkable, noteworthy (facts);

nobilitas, nobilitatis *n* (3rd) *f* nobility, noble class; (noble) birth, descent; fame, excellence; the nobles; rank;

nocturnus, nocturna, nocturnum *adi* nocturnal, of night, at night, by night;

nolo, nolle, nolui, - *v* be unwilling; wish not to; refuse to;

nomen, nominis *n* (3rd) *n* name, family name; noun; account, entry in debt ledger; sake; title, heading;

nove, novius, novissime *adv* newly, in new, unusual manner; recently, short time ago; finally, lastly; at last;

noviter *adv* recently, newly;

nox, noctis *n* (3rd) *f* night [prima nocte => early in the night; multa nocte => late at night];

nubo, nubere, nupsi, nuptus *v* (3rd) marry, be married to;

nudus, nuda, nudum *adi* nude; bare, stripped;

nunc *adv* now, today, at present;

nuncupo, nuncupare, nuncupavi,

nuncupatus *v* **(1st)** call, name; express;

nuntio, nuntiare, nuntiavi, nuntiatus *v* **(1st)** *trans* announce, report, bring word, give warning; convey, deliver, relate message, greeting;

nuntium, nunti(i) *n* **(2nd)** *n* message, announcement; news; notice of divorce, annulment of betrothal;

nutricius, nutrici(i) *n* **(2nd)** *m* tutor; foster-father;

nux, nucis *n* **(3rd)** *f* nut;

obdormio, obdormire, obdormivi, obdormitus *v* **(4th)** fall asleep;

obeo, obire, obivi(ii), obitus *v* go to meet; attend to; fall; die;

obsecro, obsecrare, obsecravi, obsecratus *v* **(1st)** *trans* entreat, beseech, implore, pray; (w, deity as object);

obses, obsidis *n* **(3rd)** **c** hostage; pledge, security;

obsideo, obsidere, obsedi, obsessus *v* **(2nd)** blockade, besiege, invest, beset; take possession of;

obtineo, obtinere, obtinui, obtentus *v* **(2nd)** get hold of; maintain; obtain; hold fast, occupy; prevail;

occidens, occidentis *n* **(3rd)** *m* west; region of the setting sun; western part of the world, its inhabitants;

occiput, occipitis *n* **(3rd)** *n* back of the head, occiput;

occisio, occisionis *n* **(3rd)** *f* murder, killing; slaughter;

occulte *adv* secretly;

occupo, occupare, occupavi, occupatus *v* **(1st)** seize; gain; overtake; capture, occupy; attack;

occuro, occurare, occuravi, occuratus *v* **(1st)** occur, come about; happen;

oculus, oculi *n* **(2nd)** *m* eye;

odium, odi(i) *n* **(2nd)** *n* hate, hatred, dislike, antipathy; odium, unpopularity; boredom, impatience; hatred (manifested by, towards group), hostility; object of hate, odium;

offero, offerare, offeravi, offeratus *v* **(1st)** offer; present; cause; bestow; (mediaeval form of offerre);

omne, omnis *n* **(3rd)** *n* all things (pl.); everything; a, the whole, entity, unit;

omnino *adv* entirely, altogether; [after negatives, with numerals => at all, in all];

onustus, onusta, onustum *adi* laden;

operatio, operationis *n* **(3rd)** *f* operation; working (of nature); activity; devotion to task; offering sacrifice; grace, work of Holy Spirit; divine service; effect, result; almsgiving, charity; surgical operation; (Cal);

oppidum, oppidi *n* **(2nd)** *n* town;

opsequium, opsequi(i) *n* **(2nd)** *n* compliance (act, form, sex, orders); consideration, deference, solicitude; services; obedience, allegiance, discipline (military); tractability, docility (animals); servility, subservience, obsequiousness; ceremony; attendance; retinue;

optimas, optimatis *n* **(3rd)** *m* aristocrat, patrician; wellborn; nobles, patricians, "Good men" adherent, partisan;

optineo, optinere, optinui, optentus *v* **(2nd)** get hold of; maintain; obtain; hold fast, occupy; prevail;

opulens, (gen.), opulentis *adi* wealthy; rich in wealth, resources; well supplied; sumptuous, opulent, rich;

opus, operis *n* **(3rd)** *n* need; work; fortifications (pl.), works; [opus est => is useful, beneficial];

ora, orae *n* **(1st)** *f* shore, coast;

oraculum, oraculi *n* **(2nd)** *n* oracle (place, agency, mouthpiece); prophecy; oracular saying, precept, maxim;

oratio, orationis *n* **(3rd)** *f* speech, oration; eloquence; prayer;

ordinarius, ordinaria, ordinarium *adi* regular, ordinary;

ordo, ordinis *n* **(3rd)** *m* row, order, rank; succession; series; class; bank (oars); order (of monks);

oriens, orientis *n* **(3rd)** *m* daybreak, dawn, sunrise; east, sunrise quarter of the sky; the East, Orient;

origo, originis *n* **(3rd)** *f* origin, source; birth, family; race; ancestry;

orior, ori, oritus sum *v* **(3rd)** *dep* rise (sun, river); arise, emerge, crop up; get up (wake); begin; originate from; be born, created; be born of, descend, spring from; proceed, be derived (from);

os, oris *n* **(3rd)** *n* mouth, speech, expression; face; pronunciation;

ostendo, ostendere, ostendi, ostensus *v* **(3rd)** show; reveal; make clear, point out, display, exhibit;

ostium, osti(i) *n* **(2nd)** *n* doorway; front door; starting gate; entrance (underworld); (river) mouth;

paciscor, pacisci, pactus sum *v* **(3rd)** *dep* make a bargain or agreement; agree, enter into a marriage contract; negotiate;

paene *adv* nearly, almost; mostly;

palatium, palati(i) *n* **(2nd)** *n* palace;

pallium, palli(i) *n* **(2nd)** *n* cover, coverlet; Greek cloak;

palus, pali *n* **(2nd)** *m* stake, pile, pole, unsplit wood; peg, pin; execution stake; wood sword; fence (pl.);

palus, paludis *n* **(3rd)** *f* swamp, marsh;

pandectes, pandectae *n* *m* encyclopedia, book of universal knowledge;

papas, papae *n* *m* Pope; tutor;

par, paris (gen.), -, parissimus -a -um *adi* equal (to); a match for; of equal size, rank, age; fit, suitable, right, proper; equal in power, prestige, importance, rank, status, office, authority; comparable; corresponding in degree, proportionate, commensurate (unlike qualities); measuring up, adequate, matching; well-matched; fair, equitable, reasonable; balanced, level; S:even, divisible by two; [~ facere => settle accounts];

paradisus, paradisi *n* **(2nd)** *m* Paradise, Garden of Eden; abode of the blessed; park, orchard; a town, river;

pareo, parere, parui, paritus *v* **(2nd)** *intrans* obey, be subject, obedient to; submit, yield, comply; pay attention; attend to; appear, be visible, be seen; be clear, evident (legal);

pariter *adv* equally; together;

pars, partis *n* **(3rd)** *f* part, region; share; direction; portion, piece; party, faction, side; role (of actor); office, function, duty (usu. pl.); [centesima ~ => 1% monthly];

partus, partus *n* **(4th)** *m* birth; offspring;

parum, minus, minime *adv* too, very little, not enough, so good, insufficient; less; (SUPER) not at all;

Pascha, Paschae *n* **(1st)** *f* Passover; Easter;

paschalis, paschalis, paschale *adi* of Easter; Paschal; of Passover;

pasco, pascere, pavi, pastus *v* **(3rd)** feed, feed on; graze;

pascua, pascuae *n* **(1st)** *f* pasture, pasture-land; piece of grazing land;

pastor, pastoris *n* **(3rd)** *m* shepherd, herdsman;

pastus, pastus *n* **(4th)** *m* pasture, feeding ground; pasturage;

pater, patris *n* **(3rd)** *m* father; [pater familias, patris familias => head of family, household];

patera, paterae *n* **(1st)** *f* bowl; saucer;

patria, patriae *n* **(1st)** *f* native land; home, native city; one's country;

patriarcha, patriarchae *n* **(1st)** *m* patriarch; father, chief of a tribe; chief bishop, Patriarch;

patriciatus, patriciatus *n* **(4th)** *m* patrician status, dignity; patriciate; dignity of imperial court;

patricius, patricii *n* **(2nd)** *m* patrician; aristocrat;

patro, patrare, patravi, patratus *v* **(1st)** accomplish, bring to completion;

paucus, pauca -um, paucior -or -us, paucissimus -a -um *adi* little, small in quantity, extent; few (usu. pl.); just a few; small number of;

paulatim *adv* little by little, by degrees, gradually; a small amount at a time, bit by bit;

paulisper *adv* for (only) a short time, brief while;

pauper, pauperis *n* **(3rd)** *m* poor man;

pavor, pavoris *n* **(3rd)** *m* fear, panic;

pax, pacis *n* **(3rd)** *f* peace; harmony;

pectus, pectoris *n* **(3rd)** *n* breast, heart; feeling, soul, mind;

peculium, peculi(i) *n* **(2nd)** *n* small savings; private property;

pecunia, pecuniae *n* **(1st)** *f* money; property;

pecus, pecudis *n* **(3rd)** *f* sheep; animal;

pellis, pellis *n* **(3rd)** *f* skin, hide; pelt;

penuria, penuriae *n* **(1st)** *f* want, need, scarcity;

perago, peragere, peregi, peractus *v* **(3rd)** disturb; finish; kill; carry through to the end, complete;

perambulo, perambulare, perambulavi, perambulatus *v* **(1st)** walk about in, tour; make the round of;

percello, percellere, perculi, perculsus *v* **(3rd)** strike down; strike; overpower; dismay, demoralize, upset;

percussor, percussoris *n* **(3rd)** *m* murderer,

assassin;

percutio, percutere, percussi, percussus *v* **(3rd)** beat, strike; pierce;

perditio, perditionis *n* **(3rd)** *f* destruction, ruin, perdition;

perduro, perdurare, perduravi, perduratus *v* **(1st)** *intrans* last long, endure;

perexiguus, perexigua, perexiguum *adi* very small;

perfero, perferre, pertuli, perlatus *v* carry through; bear, endure to the end, suffer; announce;

perfidus, perfida, perfidum *adi* faithless, treacherous, false, deceitful;

pergo, pergere, perrexi, perrectus *v* **(3rd)** go on, proceed;

perimo, perimere, peremi, peremptus *v* **(3rd)** kill, destroy;

permaneo, permanere, permansi, permansus *v* **(2nd)** last, continue; remain; endure;

pernicies, perniciei *n* **(5th)** *f* ruin; disaster; pest, bane; curse; destruction, calamity; mischief;

persequor, persequi, persecutus sum *v* **(3rd)** *dep* follow up, pursue; overtake; attack; take vengeance on; accomplish;

perseverans, perseverantis (gen.), perseverantior -or -us, perseverantissimus -a -u *adi* steadfast, persistent, untiring; continually maintained, persistent (activity);

persevero, perseverare, perseveravi, perseveratus *v* **(1st)** persist, persevere; continue;

persolvo, persolvere, persolvi, persolutus *v* **(3rd)** pay;

persono, personare, personavi, personatus *v* **(1st)** *trans* make loud, continuous, pervasive noise, loud music; ring, resound; chant, shout out;

perstringo, perstringere, perstrinxi, perstrictus *v* **(3rd)** graze, graze against; make tight all over; offend, make unfavourable mention;

persuadeo, persuadere, persuasi, persuasus *v* **(2nd)** persuade, convince (with dat.);

perterreo, perterrere, perterrui, perterritus *v* **(2nd)** *trans* frighten greatly, terrify;

pervado, pervadere, pervasi, pervasus *v*

(3rd) go or come through; spread through; penetrate; pervade;

pilum, pili *n* **(2nd)** *n* javelin, heavy iron-tipped throwing spear; pike;

piscina, piscinae *n* **(1st)** *f* pool; fishpond; swiming pool, spa; tank, vat, basln;

plaga, plagae *n* **(1st)** *f* tract, region, quarter, zone, area; open expanse of country, sea, sky;

plenus, plena -um, plenior -or -us, plenissimus -a -um *adi* full, plump; satisfied;

plerumque *adv* generally, commonly; mostly, for the most part; often, frequently;

pluvia, pluviae *n* **(1st)** *f* rain, shower;

poculum, poculi *n* **(2nd)** *n* cup, bowl, drinking vessel; drink, draught; social drinking (pl.); drink;

poena, poenae *n* **(1st)** *f* penalty, punishment; revenge, retribution; [poena dare => to pay the penalty];

pollex, pollicis *n* **(3rd)** *m* thumb;

pomus, pomi *n* **(2nd)** *f* fruit, fruit-tree;

pons, pontis *n* **(3rd)** *m* bridge;

pontifex, pontificis *n* **(3rd)** *m* high priest, pontiff; (of Roman supreme college of priests); bishop; pope;

populus, populi *n* **(2nd)** *m* people, nation, State; public, populace, multitude, crowd; a following; members of a society, sex; region, district; army;

porta, portae *n* **(1st)** *f* gate, entrance; city gates; door; avenue; goal (soccer);

portus, portus *n* **(4th)** *m* port, harbour; refuge, haven, place of refuge;

posco, poscere, poposci, - *v* **(3rd)** ask, demand;

positus, positus *n* **(4th)** *m* situation, position; arrangement;

possideo, possidere, possedi, possessus *v* **(2nd)** seize, hold, be master of; possess, take, hold possession of, occupy; inherit;

postmodum *adv* after a while, later, a little later; afterwards; presently;

postquam *coni* after;

postremum *adv* for the last time, last of all; finally;

potenter, potentius, potentissime *adv* effectively, cogently; in overbearing manner; powerfully, w, force; competently;

potentia, potentiae *n* **(1st)** *f* force, power, political power;

praebeo, praebere, praebui, praebitus *v* **(2nd)** *trans* present, show, put forward; offer; expose physically oneself; expose, submit, allow; make available, supply, provide; be the cause, occasion, produce; render;

praecaveo, praecavere, praecavi, praecautus *v* **(2nd)** guard (against), beware;

praecipue *adv* especially; chiefly;

praeda, praedae *n* **(1st)** *f* booty, loot, spoils, plunder, prey;

praefatio, praefationis *n* **(3rd)** *f* preliminary form of words, formula of announcement; preface;

praefecus, praefeci *n* **(2nd)** *m* director, president, chief, governor;

praemitto, praemittere, praemisi, praemissus *v* **(3rd)** send ahead or forward;

praenomen, praenominis *n* **(3rd)** *n* first name, personal name; noun which precedes another noun (gram.);

praeopto, praeoptare, praeoptavi, praeoptatus *v* **(1st)** prefer;

praeparo, praeparare, praeparavi, praeparatus *v* **(1st)** prepare;

praeter *prep acc* besides, except, contrary to; beyond (rank), in front of, before; more than;

praevaleo, praevalere, praevalui, - *v* **(2nd)** *intrans* prevail; have superior power, force, weight, influence, worth, efficacy (medicine);

presbiter, presbiteri *n* **(2nd)** *m* elder, presbyter (in Christian Church); priest;

pretium, preti(i) *n* **(2nd)** *n* price, value, worth; reward, pay; money; prayer, request; [~ natalis => weregeld];

pridem *adv* some time ago, previously;

primitus *adv* at first; to begin with; for the first time; originally; in the beginning;

princeps, principis *n* **(3rd)** *m* leader, chief, first, leading member, citizen, man; master, expert; founder, proposer; rinceps (non-military title of Roman Emperor); senior Senator; leader of pack;

principatus, principatus *n* **(4th)** *m* first place; rule; leadership; supremacy; chief command;

privatim *adv* in private; as a private citizen;

proavus, proavi *n* **(2nd)** *m* great-grandfather; remote ancestor;

probo, probare, probavi, probatus *v* **(1st)** *trans* approve (of), esteem, commend, recommend, certify; give assent, approval, sanction; let; show to be real, true; examine, test, try, prove, demonstrate; get accepted;

procerus, procera -um, procerior -or -us, procerissimus -a -um *adi* tall; long; high, lofty, upraised; grown, extended to great height, length;

procul *adv* away; at distance, far off;

prodigus, prodiga, prodigum *adi* wasteful, lavish, prodigal;

proditrix, proditricis *n* **(3rd)** *f* betrayer (female), treacherous woman, traitress, traitoress;

proelium, proeli(i) *n* **(2nd)** *n* battle, fight, bout, conflict, dispute; armed, hostile encounter; bout of strength;

profano, profanare, profanavi, profanatus *v* **(1st)** desecrate, profane;

proficio, proficere, profeci, profectus *v* **(3rd)** make, accomplish, effect;

proficiscor, proficisci, profectus sum *v* **(3rd)** *dep* depart, set out; proceed;

profundo, profundere, profudi, profusus *v* **(3rd)** pour, pour out; utter; squander;

profundus, profunda, profundum *adi* deep, profound; boundless; insatiable;

progredior, progredi, progressus sum *v* **(3rd)** *dep* go, come forth, go forward, march forward; advance. proceed. make progress;

prohibeo, prohibere, prohibui, prohibitus *v* **(2nd)** hinder, restrain; forbid, prevent;

prolixitas, prolixitatis *n* **(3rd)** *f* extent; extension in space, elongation; extension in time, long duration;

promereo, promerere, promerui, promeritus *v* **(2nd)** deserve, merit; deserve well of; earn; gain;

promissio, promissionis *n* **(3rd)** *f* promise; act, instance of promising; guarantee that proof will come (rhetoric);

promitto, promittere, promisi, promissus *v* **(3rd)** promise;

pronuntio, pronuntiare, pronuntiavi, pronuntiatus *v* **(1st)** announce; proclaim; relate; divulge; recite; utter;

propaganda, propagandae *n* **(1st)** *f* propaganda;

propago, propagare, propagavi, propagatus *v* **(1st)** propagate; extend, enlarge, increase;

prope *prep acc* near;

prophetia, prophetiae *n* **(1st)** *f* prophecy; prediction; body of prophets, singers;

propinquus, propinqui *n* **(2nd)** *m* relative;

proprius, propria, proprium *adi* own, very own; individual; special, particular, characteristic;

propter *prep acc* near; on account of; by means of; because of;

prospicio, prospicere, prospexi, prospectus *v* **(3rd)** foresee; see far off; watch for, provide for, look out for;

prosterno, prosternere, prostravi, prostratus *v* **(3rd)** *trans* knock over, lay low; strike down, overthrow; exhaust; debase, demean; prostrate;

prosum, prodesse, profui, profuturus *v* be useful, be advantageous, benefit, profit (with *dat*);

prout *adv* just as; as; according to;

proximus, proxima, proximum *adi* nearest, closest, next; most recent, immediately preceding, last; most, very like;

puella, puellae *n* **(1st)** *f* girl, (female) child, daughter; maiden; young woman, wife; sweetheart; slavegirl;

puer, pueri *n* **(2nd)** *m* boy, lad, young man; servant; (male) child; [a puere => from boyhood];

puerilis, puerilis, puerile *adi* boyish; youthful, childish;

puerulus, pueruli *n* **(2nd)** *m* little boy;

pugna, pugnae *n* **(1st)** *f* battle, fight;

pugno, pugnare, pugnavi, pugnatus *v* **(1st)** fight; dispute; [pugnatum est => the battle raged];

pullus, pulli *n* **(2nd)** *m* chicken, young hen;

pungo, pungere, pepugi, punctus *v* **(3rd)** *trans* prick, puncture; sting (insect); jab, poke; mark with points, pricks; vex, trouble;

puto, putare, putavi, putatus *v* **(1st)** *trans* think, believe, suppose, hold; reckon, estimate, value; clear up, settle;

putrefacio, putrefacere, putrefeci, putrefactus *v* **(3rd)** *trans* cause to rot, decay, crumble, disintegrate; putrefy; make friable; soften;

quaero, quaerere, quaesivi, quaesitus *v* **(3rd)** search for, seek, strive for; obtain; ask, inquire, demand;

qualis, qualis, quale *adi* what kind, sort, condition (of); what is (he, it) like; what, how excellent a ...;

quamvis *coni* however much; although;

quando *coni* when, since, because; [si quando => if ever];

quandoque *adv* whenever, at whatever time; at some time or other, any time, ever; whereas;

quantocius *adv* the sooner, quicker the better;

quantum *adv* so much as; how much; how far;

quia *coni* because;

quippe *adv* of course; as you see; obviously; naturally; by all means;

quomodo *adv* how, in what way; just as;

quotiens *adv* how often; as often as;

rabies, rabiei *n* **(5th)** *f* madness;

radius, radi(i) *n* **(2nd)** *m* ray; rod;

rapina, rapinae *n* **(1st)** *f* robbery, plunder, booty; rape;

rapio, rapere, rapui, raptus *v* **(3rd)** drag off; snatch; destroy; seize, carry off; pillage; hurry;

ratio, rationis *n* **(3rd)** *f* account, reckoning, invoice; plan; prudence; method; reasoning; rule; regard;

reaedifico, reaedificare, reaedificavi, reaedificatus *v* **(1st)** *re*build, reconstruct, remake; recreate; reestablish;

rebellio, rebellionis *n* **(3rd)** *f* rebellion;

rebello, rebellare, rebellavi, rebellatus *v* **(1st)** rebel, revolt;

recedo, recedere, recessi, recessus *v* **(3rd)** recede, go back, withdraw, ebb; retreat; retire; move, keep, pass, slip away;

reconditus, recondita, reconditum *adi* hidden, concealed; abstruse;

recondo, recondere, recondidi, reconditus *v* **(3rd)** hide, conceal; put away;

refero, referre, rettuli, relatus *v* bring, carry back, again, home; move, draw, force back, withdraw; go back, return; report (on), bring back news; record, enter; propose, open debate; assign, count; give, pay back, render, tender; restore; redirect; revive, repeat; recall;

regio, regionis *n* **(3rd)** *f* area, region; neighbourhood; district, country; direction;

regius, regia, regium *adi* royal, of a king, regal;

regno, regnare, regnavi, regnatus *v* **(1st)** reign, rule; be king; play the lord, be master;

regnum, regni *n* **(2nd)** *n* royal power;

power; control; kingdom;

rego, regere, rexi, rectus *v* **(3rd)** rule, guide; manage, direct;

regredior, regredi, regressus sum *v* **(3rd)** *dep* go back, return, retreat;

relego, relegare, relegavi, relegatus *v* **(1st)** banish, remove; relegate;

relictus, relicta -um, relictior -or -us, relictissimus -a -um *adi* forsaken, abandoned, derelict; left untouched;

religio, religionis *n* **(3rd)** *f* supernatural constraint, taboo; obligation; sanction; worship; rite; sanctity; reverence, respect, awe, conscience, scruples; religion; order of monks, nuns;

relinquo, relinquere, reliqui, relictus *v* **(3rd)** leave behind, abandon; (pass.) be left, remain; bequeath;

reliquus, reliqua, reliquum *adi* rest of, remaining, available, left; surviving; future, further; yet to be, owed;

reperio, reperire, repperi, repertus *v* **(4th)** *trans* discover, learn; light on; find, obtain, get; find out, to be, get to know; invent;

repperio, repperire, repperi, reppertus *v* **(4th)** *trans* discover, learn; light on; find, obtain, get; find out, to be, get to know; invent;

repugno, repugnare, repugnavi, repugnatus *v* **(1st)** fight back, oppose; be incompatible with; disagree with;

requiro, requirere, requisivi, requisitus *v* **(3rd)** require, seek, ask for; need; miss, pine for;

res, rei *n* **(5th)** *f* thing; event, affair, business; fact; cause; property; [~ familiaris => property];

resideo, residere, resedi, resessus *v* **(2nd)** sit down, on, in; settle; be perched; remain seated, idle, fixed, in place; squat; abate, subside; be left over, retained, persist, stay; fall back;

resisto, resistere, restiti, - *v* **(3rd)** pause; continue; resist, oppose; reply; withstand, stand (*dat*); make a stand;

restauro, restaurare, restauravi, restauratus *v* **(1st)** *trans* restore (condition); rebuild; bring back, re-establish, take up again; renew;

retego, retegere, retexi, retectus *v* **(3rd)** uncover, lay bare, reveal, disclose;

retineo, retinere, retinui, retentus *v* **(2nd)** hold back, restrain; uphold; delay; hold fast; retain, preserve;

rex, regis *n* **(3rd)** *m* king;

rupes, rupis *n* **(3rd)** *f* cliff; rock;

rursus *adv* turned back, backward; on the contrary, other hand, in return, in turn, again;

saeculum, saeculi *n* **(2nd)** *n* age; generation, people born at a time; breed, race; present time, age; century;

saepe, saepius, saepissime *adv* often, oft, oftimes, many times, frequently;

saevitia, saevitiae *n* **(1st)** *f* rage, fierceness, ferocity; cruelty, barbarity, violence;

sagitta, sagittae *n* **(1st)** *f* arrow;

salio, salire, salivi, saltus *v* **(4th)** leap, jump; move suddenly, spasmodically (part of body under stress), twitch; spurt, discharge, be ejected under force (water, fluid); mount, cover (by stud);

saltus, saltus *n* **(4th)** *m* leap, spring, jump; stage, step;

sane *adv* reasonably, sensibly; certainly, truly; however; yes, of course;

sanguis, sanguinis *n* **(3rd)** *m* blood; family;

saturitas, saturitatis *n* **(3rd)** *f* fullness, satiety (food, drink); surplus of digested food; abundance, plenitude; condition of being imbued with a colour to saturation;

scabellum, scabelli *n* **(2nd)** *n* footstool; a musical instrument played with the foot;

scala, scalae *n* **(1st)** *f* ladder (pl.);

scio, scire, scivi, scitus *v* **(4th)** *trans* know, understand;

scribo, scribere, scripsi, scriptus *v* **(3rd)** write; compose;

secedo, secedere, secessi, secessus *v* **(3rd)** withdraw; rebel; secede;

sedeo, sedere, sedi, sessus *v* **(2nd)** sit, remain; settle; encamp;

sedes, sedis *n* **(3rd)** *f* seat; home, residence; settlement, habitation; chair;

seges, segetis *n* **(3rd)** *f* grain field; crop;

sella, sellae *n* **(1st)** *f* seat (usu. no back, arms), stool, chair; chair of magistrate, office, teacher; sedan, carrying chair; toilet seat, stool; work-stool; coach, wagon seat; saddle;

senex, senis *n* **(3rd)** *m* old man;

sepelio, sepelire, sepelivi, sepultus *v* **(4th)** *trans* bury, inter; (Romans cremate + inter ashes); submerge, overcome; suppress; ruin;

sermo, sermonis *n* **(3rd)** *m* conversation,

discussion; rumor; diction; speech; talk; the word;

servo, servare, servavi, servatus *v* **(1st)** watch over; protect, store, keep, guard, preserve, save;

sessio, sessionis *n* **(3rd)** *f* sitting; session;

siccitas, siccitatis *n* **(3rd)** *f* dryness; drought; dried up condition;

sicut *adv* as, just as; like; in same way; as if; as it certainly is; as it were;

signaculum, signaculi *n* **(2nd)** *n* seal;

signum, signi *n* **(2nd)** *n* battle standard; indication; seal; sign, proof; signal; image, statue;

silentium, silenti(i) *n* **(2nd)** *n* silence;

sin *coni* but if; if on the contrary;

sine *prep abl* without; (sometimes after object);

sinodus, sinodi *n* **(2nd)** *m* synod, general council; book of synodal acts, constituions;

siquidem *coni* accordingly; if indeed, in fact, it is possible, even supposing; since, in that;

socer, soceri *n* **(2nd)** *m* father in law;

sol, solis *n* **(3rd)** *m* sun;

solitudo, solitudinis *n* **(3rd)** *f* solitude, loneliness; deprivation; wilderness;

solummodo *adv* only, just, merely, barely, alone; [nonsolum ...sed etiam => not only ...but also];

solus, sola, solum (gen -ius) *adi* only, single; lonely; alone, having no companion, friend, protector; unique;

solutus, soluta -um, solutior -or -us, solutissimus -a -um *adi* unbound, released; free, at large; unrestrained, profligate; lax, careless;

solvo, solvere, solvi, solutus *v* **(3rd)** loosen, release, unbind, untie, free; open; set sail; scatter; pay off, back;

somnus, somni *n* **(2nd)** *m* sleep;

sopor, soporis *n* **(3rd)** *m* deep sleep;

sordes, sordis *n* **(3rd)** *f* filth, dirt, uncleanness, squalor; meanness, stinginess; humiliation, baseness;

soror, sororis *n* **(3rd)** *f* sister; (applied also to half sister, sister-in-law, and mistress!);

sors, sortis *n* **(3rd)** *f* lot, fate; oracular response;

spes, spei *n* **(5th)** *f* hope, anticipation, expectation; prospect, hope, promise; (inheriting, succeeding); object,

embodiment of hope; hope personified;

spiritus, spiritus *n* **(4th)** *m* breath, breathing, air, soul, life;

statura, staturae *n* **(1st)** *f* height, stature;

stella, stellae *n* **(1st)** *f* star; planet, heavenly body; point of light in jewel; constellation; star shape;

stilus, stili *n* **(2nd)** *m* stylus, iron pen; column, pillar;

stirps, stirpis *n* **(3rd)** *f* race;

sto, stare, steti, status *v* **(1st)** stand, stand still, stand firm; remain, rest;

strages, stragis *n* **(3rd)** *f* overthrow; massacre, slaughter, cutting down; havoc; confused heap;

studeo, studere, studui, - *v* **(2nd)** desire, be eager for; busy oneself with; strive;

studium, studi(i) *n* **(2nd)** *n* eagerness, enthusiasm, zeal, spirit; devotion, pursuit, study;

stuprum, stupri *n* **(2nd)** *n* dishonour, shame; (illicit) sexual intercourse;

subito *adv* suddenly, unexpectedly; at once, at short notice, quickly; in no time at all;

subsequor, subsequi, subsecutus sum *v* **(3rd)** *dep* follow close after; pursue; support;

subter *prep abl* beneath, under (cover, shelter); towards, at base (of wall, cliff); (usu. *acc*);

subtraho, subtrahere, subtraxi, subtractus *v* **(3rd)** carry off; take away; subtract;

succurro, succurrere, succucurri, succursus *v* **(3rd)** run to the aid of, help;

suffero, sufferre, sustuli, sublatus *v* bear, endure, suffer;

sumo, sumere, sumpsi, sumptus *v* **(3rd)** take up; begin; suppose, assume; select; purchase; exact (punishment); obtain;

superbus, superba, superbum *adi* arrogant, overbearing, haughty, proud;

supero, superare, superavi, superatus *v* **(1st)** overcome, conquer; survive; outdo; surpass, be above, have the upper hand;

supervenio, supervenire, superveni, superventus *v* **(4th)** come up, arrive;

supplicatio, supplicationis *n* **(3rd)** *f* thanksgiving; supplication;

supplico, supplicare, supplicavi, supplicatus *v* **(1st)** pray, supplicate; humbly beseech;

supra *prep acc* above, beyond; over; more than; in charge of, in authority over;

sustineo, sustinere, sustinui, sustentus *v* **(2nd)** support; check; put off; put up with; sustain; hold back;

talis, talis, tale *adi* such; so great; so excellent; of such kind;

taliter *adv* in such a manner, way (as described), so;

tandem *adv* finally; at last, in the end; after some time, eventually; at length;

tantummodo *adv* only, merely;

tantus, tanta, tantum *adi* of such size; so great, so much; [tantus ... quantus => as much ... as];

tela, telae *n* **(1st)** *f* web; warp (threads that run lengthwise in the loom);

telum, teli *n* **(2nd)** *n* dart, spear; weapon, javelin;

tempestas, tempestatis *n* **(3rd)** *f* season, time, weather; storm;

tempus, temporis *n* **(3rd)** *n* time, condition, right time; season, occasion; necessity;

tenus *prep abl* as far as, to the extent of, up to, down to;

testor, testari, testatus sum *v* **(1st)** *dep* give as evidence; bear witness; make a will; swear; testify;

thesaurus, thesauri *n* **(2nd)** *m* treasure chamber, vault, repository; treasure; hoard; collected precious objects;

timor, timoris *n* **(3rd)** *m* fear; dread;

tollo, tollere, sustuli, sublatus *v* **(3rd)** *trans* lift, raise; destroy; remove, steal; take, lift up, away;

tonitrus, tonitrus *n* **(4th)** *m* thunder;

trado, tradere, tradidi, traditus *v* **(3rd)** hand over, surrender; deliver; bequeath; relate;

transgredior, transgredi, transgressus sum *v* **(3rd)** *dep* cross, go, move, travel over, across; go to other side; change allegiance, policy;

triduum, tridui *n* **(2nd)** *n* three days;

tueor, tueri, tuitus sum *v* **(2nd)** *dep* see, look at; protect, watch; uphold;

tumulus, tumuli *n* **(2nd)** *m* mound, hillock; mound, tomb;

tunc *adv* then, thereupon, at that time;

turbo, turbare, turbavi, turbatus *v* **(1st)** disturb, agitate, throw into confusion;

ubertas, ubertatis *n* **(3rd)** *f* fruitfulness, fertility; abundance, plenty;

ubi *coni* where, whereby;

ubique *adv* anywhere, everywhere (ubiquitous);

ultra, ulterius, ultimum *adv* beyond, further; on the other side; more, more than, in addition, besides;

unde *adv* from where, whence, from what or which place; from which; from whom;

undique *adv* from every side, direction, place, part, source; on all, both sides, surfaces; everywhere; completely; allover; from every point of view, in all respects;

unus -a -um, primus -a -um, singuli -ae -a, semel *num* one;

urbs, urbis *n* **(3rd)** *f* city;

utor, uti, usus sum *v* **(3rd)** *dep* use, make use of, enjoy; enjoy the friendship of (with *abl*);

utpote *adv* as, in as much as; namely; inasmuch as;

uxor, uxoris *n* **(3rd)** *f* wife;

vagina, vaginae *n* **(1st)** *f* sheath, scabbard;

valde, valdius, valdissime *adv* greatly, very, intensely; vigorously, strongly, powerfully, energetically; loudly;

valeo, valere, valui, valitus *v* **(2nd)** be strong, powerful, influential, healthy; prevail;

validus, valida, validum *adi* strong, powerful; valid;

vanitas, vanitatis *n* **(3rd)** *f* emptiness, untruthfulness; futility, foolishness, empty pride;

vas, vasis *n* **(3rd)** *n* vessel, dish; vase; pack, kit; utensil, instrument, tool; equipment, apparatus (pl.);

vasto, vastare, vastavi, vastatus *v* **(1st)** lay waste, ravage, devastate;

vastus, vasta -um, vastior -or -us, vastissimus -a -um *adi* huge, vast; monstrous;

velociter, velocius, velocissime *adv* swiftly, rapidly, with speed of movement; quickly, in a short time;

venabulum, venabuli *n* **(2nd)** *n* hunting-spear;

veneratio, venerationis *n* **(3rd)** *f* veneration, reverence, worship;

venio, venire, veni, ventus *v* **(4th)** come;

vero *adv* yes; in truth; certainly; truly, to be sure; however;

verro, verrere, verri, versus *v* **(3rd)** sweep clean; sweep together; sweep (to the ground); skim, sweep; sweep along;

verus, vera -um, verior -or -us, verissimus -a -um *adi* true, real, genuine, actual; properly named; well founded; right, fair, proper;

vestiaria, vestiariae n **(1ˢᵗ)** *f* dressing-maid;

vestigium, vestigi(i) *n* **(2nd)** *n* step, track; trace; footstep;

vestimentum, vestimenti *n* **(2nd)** *n* garment, robe; clothes;

vestio, vestire, vestivi, vestitus *v* **(4th)** clothe;

vicinus, vicina, vicinum *adi* nearby, neighbouring;

video, videre, vidi, visus *v* **(2nd)** see, look at; consider; (*passive*) seem, seem good, appear, be seen;

viduus, vidua, viduum *adi* widowed, deprived of (with gen.); bereft; unmarried;

vilis, vilis, vile *adi* cheap, common, mean, worthless;

villa, villae *n* **(1st)** *f* farm, country home, estate; large country residence, seat, villa; village;

vindico, vindicare, vindicavi, vindicatus *v* **(1st)** claim, vindicate; punish, avenge;

vinum, vini *n* **(2nd)** *n* wine;

violentia, violentiae *n* **(1st)** *f* violence, aggressiveness;

vir, viri *n* **(2nd)** *m* man; husband; hero; person of courage, honour, and nobility;

virgo, virginis *n* **(3rd)** *f* maiden, young woman, girl of marriageable age; virgin, woman sexually intact;

viriliter, virilius, virilissime *adv* with masculine, manly vigour; manfully, in a manly, virile way; powerfully;

virtus, virtutis *n* **(3rd)** *f* strength, power; courage, bravery; worth, manliness, virtue, character, excellence; army; host; mighty works (pl.); class of Angels;

viscer, visceris *n* **(3rd)** *n* entrails; innermost part of the body; heart; vitals;

vita, vitae *n* **(1st)** *f* life, career, livelihood; mode of life;

vivo, vivere, vixi, victus *v* **(3rd)** be alive, live; survive; reside;

vix *adv* hardly, scarcely, barely, only just; with difficulty, not easily; reluctantly;

voco, vocare, vocavi, vocatus *v* **(1st)** call, summon; name; call upon;

volo, velle, volui, - *v* wish, want, prefer; be willing, will;

voluntas, voluntatis *n* **(3rd)** *f* will, desire; purpose; good will; wish, favour, consent;

vulgus, vulgi *n* **(2nd)** *n* common people, general public, multitude, common herd, rabble, crowd, mob; flock;

CPSIA information can be obtained
at www.ICGtesting.com
Printed in the USA
LVHW041000170423
744543LV00012B/542

9 781719 512596